# BUCKLE
# UP
# BUTTERCUP!

## HOW TO DRIVE SUCCESS BY
## EMBRACING THE POWER OF CHANGE

# PRAISE FOR
# *BUCKLE UP, BUTTERCUP!*

"Buckle Up, Buttercup! is loaded with inspirational insights that will arm the readers with tools to face the changes coming in their lives! Michelle weaves compelling stories of her life with the reality of the uncertainty ahead. We all become complacent, and we accept the current situation of our lives as unchangeable because of our fear of the unknown. Michelle's own experience to break from a circumstance in which she felt trapped in her career provides encouragement, and upon reflection, the reader will see change as opportunity versus risks of the unknown. I appreciate Michelle's perspectives, as they come from a generational point-of-view that is different than mine yet loaded with wisdom that crosses boundaries. I recommend Buckle Up, Buttercup! as an entertaining, yet thoughtful, tool that readers will revisit to re-energize and confidently embrace the opportunities of change."

**Carson Sublett**
Speaker, Coach, Entrepreneur, Pharmaceutical Operations Expert, and Author of Bosses Are Hired, Leadership Is Earned: Experiences. Lessons. Decisions. Life.

"Life can be a bumpy road, full of potholes and unexpected twists and turns. Michelle Wyatt takes the reader on this wild journey, providing insights for how to make the most of change — both personal and professional. In her engaging style, she invites readers to grab the wheel with both hands! End-of-chapter questions provide space for reflection and discussion. Highly recommended!"

**Cathy Fyock**
Author, *The Speaker Author: Sell More Books and Book More Speeches*


"*Buckle Up, Buttercup!* is a must-read, go-to resource for change! Michelle delivers real-life examples and asks thought-provoking questions while addressing with compassion the common fears and experiences we often face when encountering uncertainty with both expected and unexpected change. Her words are a companion, and an inspiring and welcoming reminder that we can embrace our emotions, find courage in our hearts, and take charge of our choices … and we are never alone. Her book is a gift I will be sharing with others for years to come."

**Penny Tate**
Mental Health Specialist, Educator, and Co-Author of Manifesting Your Dreams: Inspiring Words of Encouragement, Strength, and Perseverance


"No one knows the struggle and difficulty of 'change' more than Michelle. But as with everything she does in life, she attacks these hurdles and life-altering moments with class. She is a true inspiration and her life story is a testimony of how to positively embrace the power of change."

**Jenna Wainer**
Owner of Morgans and Lakeland Funeral Homes

"*Buckle Up, Buttercup!* is written by one of the sweetest and most full-of-life individuals I know. Michelle's voice definitely comes to life in this book as I read her real-life story examples and experiences of embracing change. I couldn't help but chuckle as I literally felt Michelle's sweet southern sass, kind and sincere heart, and love for people and life jump off the pages. It's a great book with practical challenges! We all owe a debt of gratitude to Michelle for writing this thought-provoking and fun book. She makes me a better me. And for readers who may never meet her, she'll make you stronger too."

**Suzanne Short**
Chief Operating Officer of Shared Services, First Southern Bancorp

"Among all things we may encounter in life, change is the most inevitable. It's under many rocks, around lots of turns and, many times, it comes when we least expect it. You may not get the choice on if change will happen, but you get the choice on how to look at the change you are experiencing. Michelle's book reminds us that embracing change will not only help us grow personally and professionally, but it just may be the driving force to guide us to our next calling."

**Stephanie Feger**
Author of *Color Today Pretty: An Inspirational Guide to Living a Life in Perspective* and Owner, Founder and Chief Strategist of emPower PR Group

"Michelle and I have worked together and grown together. But more importantly, we have learned how to change into leaders who are adaptable. Change is difficult and great leaders are reflective, as they must learn about themselves to be effective. In this book, Michelle tackles how to approach change — one of the biggest parts of your development."

**Alex Keltner**
President, First Southern National Bank

"I have always believed that life is about choices. As was once said to me many years ago, 'Everything in life can make you bitter or better ... it is up to you to choose.' For many years, I have given the advice to my own children and other young people, 'Be prepared to change on anything and everything — except your principles and values.' Because in my own life I have observed that the happiest and most successful folks are the ones who truly embrace change but stick to their core values. Michelle's book provides a roadmap for how to reflect and make changes in your own life so you can maximize and have a life well lived. I have had the privilege of working with Michelle, a very gifted lady, for many years and have watched her use her life to help others deal with challenges and make changes that are needed to live life to the fullest."

**James P. Rousey**
CEO of First Southern Bancorp, and President of UTG Insurance


"In times of uncertainty, one thing is certain. Change. As a woman entrepreneur, when I decided what mattered most was me, my biggest fear became fear of not taking the greatest risks. In her remarkable book, *Buckle Up, Buttercup!*, Michelle Wyatt beautifully takes us through her own personal journey of life's twists and turns and she provides a framework of tools to understanding the incredible lessons change can give us. This book is for all of us who have found ourselves at a crossroads in life and are looking for a simple and powerful approach to getting comfortable with the uncomfortable ... so that we can love the lives we live."

**Janel Dyan**
Founder and CEO of Janel Dyan, Inc., Speaker and Author of *Story. Style. Brand.: Why Corporate Results Are a Matter of Personal Style*

"Parents, teachers, coaches, employers, employees, and individuals alike ... Michelle Wyatt, in her unique and Southern way, takes you on a journey in *Buckle Up, Buttercup!* — a journey you will be grateful to have taken, and will inevitably want to embrace and share."

**Lanie Gardner**
Community President, First Southern National Bank, Central City, KY

"'Embracing even the most uncertain changes can often lead to beautiful destinations ...' was one of the many lines that resonated with me while reading *Buckle Up, Buttercup!* As a mother who had to advocate and pave a new way for my special-needs son and family, I too faced the big moment in life when the world turned upside down and I was left to either pick up the pieces or sit among them. I would have given anything to have had Michelle Wyatt's book in my hands back then! I feel confident it would have emboldened me more quickly to realize I had the power of *choice* and that I could choose to *embrace* the change. We cannot control life's many detours, whether personal or professional, but we can control how we *react* to those changes. We can invest our energy in relationships and positive opportunities and still come out on top! *Buckle Up, Buttercup!* does not disappoint; it teaches us that if you embrace change, you embrace life."

**Rebecca Duvall Scott**
Author of *Sensational Kids, Sensational Families: Hope for Sensory Processing Differences*, Speaker and Intervention Strategist

"What perfect timing for a book about change, as we adjust to a post-pandemic new normal. Michelle uses life experience, humor, and relationships to better prepare readers of all ages to make the most of the opportunities presented by change — opportunities that many times are missed or ignored."

**Susan Wells**
Deposit Manager, First Southern National Bank

# MICHELLE WYATT

# BUCKLE UP BUTTERCUP!

## HOW TO DRIVE SUCCESS BY EMBRACING THE POWER OF CHANGE

SILVER TREE PUBLISHING

*Buckle Up, Buttercup! How to Drive Success by*
*Embracing the Power of Change*

Copyright 2020 by Michelle Wyatt

Published by Silver Tree Publishing,
a division of Silver Tree Communications, LLC (Kenosha, WI).
www.SilverTreePublishing.com

All rights reserved. No portion of this book may be reproduced, scanned,
sold, or distributed in any printed or electronic form without the express
written permission of the author.

This book contains several true stories, from the author's own life and
from the lives and careers of others. Some names and minor details
have been changed to honor the privacy of others. Poems that appear at
chapter beginnings are the original creative work of Michelle Wyatt.

Editing by:
Kate Colbert

Cover design and typesetting by:
Lorenne Marketing & Design

First edition, May 2020

ISBN: 978-1-948238-28-1

Library of Congress Control Number: 2020903671

Created in the United States of America

# DEDICATION

This book is dedicated to my sons, Cole and Case. The journey of navigating motherhood is the greatest blessing I have ever known.

# TABLE OF CONTENTS

# LETTER TO THE READER

If there was one universal principle that you could embrace to make your entire life easier ... would you?

If that principle or mindset could transform your career, improve your personal life, and help you achieve your goals, would you commit yourself to it, even if doing so was hard at first or didn't come to you naturally?

Well, *Buckle Up, Buttercup,* because the one thing you need to embrace — at home and at work — is CHANGE! And change is hard. But fear not. Just as most of us learned to drive a car (going from nervous amateur to practiced expert), you can learn to drive *success* by embracing the power of change. And I'm here to teach you the rules of the road and the safety features of your vehicle, so don't be afraid.

---

**You can learn to drive success by embracing the power of change.**

---

If you're like most people, you're thinking, *"You're crazy, Michelle! Nobody loves change. How can even the most insightful, encouraging book teach me to welcome change?"* By and large, we're not hardwired to embrace change — we resist it. Because change (even positive change) is hard for individuals and teams everywhere. Humans like predictability and routine. And even when life or work is not going well, it's not unusual to resist the changes that might make things better.

Take, for example, working at a job you don't love, where your manager is unfriendly or where the paycheck isn't what you think you deserve. Your friends or spouse might encourage you to "just find a new job if you're not happy" but you might find yourself thinking along the lines of the old proverb about choosing "the devil we know versus the devil we don't know." The unknown — even if it might bring rewards, happiness and peace — is still scary to most of us because experiencing the unknown means experiencing change.

# WELCOME TO THE JOURNEY

What happens when the things you thought you *wanted* — like your initial college major, your dream job, your relationships or family structure, your new home — turn out wrong? How do you cope when life doesn't go as planned? Are you able to course-correct and make the necessary changes to try something new or better?

How do you handle unwelcomed changes at work or at home? Do you embrace them or resist them?

Do you achieve the goals you set for yourself, no matter how hard the work is, or do you feel like you spend most days spinning your wheels, living in the ho-hum of the status quo?

Change can take you on a wild journey. There are twists, turns, bumpy roads and sometimes the car breaks down. Just know that you are not alone. I encourage you to use this book as a guide to embrace, navigate, and leverage change in personal and professional settings. Being able to embrace change when others have difficulty can make you stand out in a crowd and showcase skills that may have otherwise been overlooked. My hope is that this book will inspire you to channel your fears into courage and conviction that push you forward by making the most of whatever change you may be facing.

## Channel your fears into courage and conviction.

**Reaching your destination doesn't happen overnight.** In each chapter of this book, we'll discuss what makes all change — even positive, worthwhile change — difficult and we'll explore ways to turn difficulty into drive. In each chapter, we'll draw connections between organizational or workplace change and your personal life. When you hear phrases like "change management" or "managing change," you might immediately think about your career. But I want this book to help you on a personal level as well. We'll explore common themes and we'll practice them. At the end of each chapter, you'll have the opportunity to take what you've learned and put it into action through practical exercises.

*Buckle Up, Buttercup!* is a practical guide you can use individually or in group settings. Use this book as a companion through organizational change or for your own personal development. Think of this book as a map to help you navigate whatever change you're facing.

Ultimately, this book was designed to be a tool. You can read it straight through or you can dive into any chapter independently if the chapter title appeals to you. Every chapter is also designed to be revisited over time, whenever you need it, because change is *constant*. Once you've successfully navigated one change, another will emerge. Use this book and the "Pit Stop" activities over and over, no matter what you are facing. It will prepare your mindset for whatever your journey brings, and keep you tethered to the principle that change is the pathway to progress.

It is my sincere hope that, after reading this book, you will begin to see change as a *good* thing — full of opportunity and silver linings — and that wherever you are, this book helps you enjoy the ride and get where you want to go ... safely, in style, and making good time.

# INTRODUCTION

---

# Buckle Up, Buttercup!

Change means something a little different to everyone, and the very idea of change can conjure a variety of emotions. You see, we all have a slightly different default relationship with change. Some of us regard change as a welcome journey while others see it as a bumpy, dangerous road. It can be both.

Several years ago, I came up against the largest decision of my entire career — an opportunity to leap or languish. The need for change in my career threatened to be something heavy, concerning, and dastardly should I navigate it incorrectly. But many, many years before that, I had learned a little something about change during a chance encounter with a corn worm.

# LEARNING TO SLOW DOWN

When I was young, I would often spend summer afternoons shucking corn with my great-grandparents on their farm in Western Kentucky. It was a wonderful way to spend an afternoon and, when it was balmy and hot, the porch swing would provide just enough of a breeze. My great-grandparents would stack bushel baskets of corn all around the porch, strewn about our feet and stacked high. Some baskets were full of corn that was waiting to be shucked while other baskets were full of shucked corn, clean and ready to prepare for cooking or freezing.

I recall one summer afternoon that was especially nice. I was 9 years old and sitting on the front porch, where both of my great-grandparents were able to sit and swing a spell. Mammaw had taught me exactly how to shuck the corn and I, per usual, was flying through my task, trying to get as many ears of corn finished as quickly as possible. I had really gotten into the zone and had convinced myself that I was the best corn shucker of all time.

Unfortunately, I hadn't considered any possible hiccups in the corn-shucking process. I went faster and faster until suddenly, POW! My right arm felt like I had been struck by lightning. I hopped up from the swing, jumped up and down, screamed, cried and did everything I could think of to make the pain go away. All the while I was suffering and panicked, my Pappaw was laughing harder than I had ever seen him laugh. My sweet Mammaw was consoling me and assuring me that I was fine, but Pappaw was still doubled over in laughter.

I was convinced that I had been electrocuted by a corn cob. Once I had calmed down enough to be coherent, my Pappaw nudged over a little, white, fuzzy and feathery looking caterpillar. It was cute. I may have even tried to touch it again, deliberately this time, had I not already been victimized by its sting. Now that he wasn't doubled over in laughter, my Pappaw had a short but sweet nugget of wisdom for me:

"I bet you look for those from now on."

And he was right. I have never since shucked corn without taking my time and making sure the cobs and husks were free of corn worms. I have slowed down and become more deliberate, keeping an eye on my own safety. As a result, I do a much better job; by slowing down, I learned not only to prevent personal injury but the change in process and attitude resulted cobs that are completely clean and ready to prepare for cooking of freezing. That's the amazing thing about change. It's almost always uncomfortable and some-times it's downright miserable, but we always grow, learn and benefit from it.

---

That's the amazing thing about change. It's almost always uncomfortable and sometimes it's downright miserable, but we always grow, learn and benefit from it.

---

## THE ROAD LESS TRAVELED

It's been a long time since I was 9 years old, and my encounters with change have, well, changed. I've endured and enjoyed hundreds of changes — some changes I've chosen for myself and others I had no control over. When I look at change holistically and recall the changes I've personally experienced as well as all the lessons I've learned about change by watching people around me, one thing is clear to me. Perhaps it is a universal truth. Change is almost never easy. In fact, it can be downright painful. When it's painful or difficult, it's almost always emotionally painful. But it can be literally painful too, like with childbirth or bodybuilding. Or it can be an emotionally painful process. With or without profound pain, change and what we learn from it is most always deeply worthwhile. It is worthwhile personally as you reach to attain goals and make dreams come to life. And it is especially valuable as it applies to careers and personal development.

---

**Perhaps it is a universal truth. Change is almost never easy. In fact, it can be downright painful.**

---

It has always fascinated me that the one constant in life — change — is also the one thing that people tend to resist the most. I've also observed that when embraced, navigated, and leveraged successfully, the process of change can lead to great opportunities and achievements for individuals and teams. Most people avoid change like the plague. They hunker down, put their heads in the sand, and resist all change that comes their way. They are rooted in their ways, comfortable with the status quo. Good enough is good enough. Eventually, they stop growing all together. They become statues watching life pass them by. They're crippled by their fears.

As you read through each chapter of this book, I want to challenge you to explore the road less traveled. To consider whatever change you are facing, chosen or not, and use each chapter of this book to explore your perception, mindset, and resulting behaviors. You may be headed straight for uncharted territory and that's okay! Sometimes when we keep going despite feeling the most lost, we find something better than we ever thought possible. Embracing even the most uncertain changes can often lead to beautiful destinations.

When my husband, Seth, and I were dating, we liked to hike together
— a great way to be together and be outside. We grew up in Western
Kentucky, where there is no shortage of wooded trails, lakes, and
beautiful surroundings. As winter was bleeding into spring, we
headed to a local nature preserve to go hiking. It was a beautiful day,
the sun was shining, and there was the slightest breeze in the air. It
was cool but, for the first time in a while, warm enough to enjoy the
outdoors. We hopped out of the truck and set off on an adventure,
noting that the ground was a little wet from rain earlier in the week.
"Let's try a different trail," Seth said. I was a little bit skeptical, but
he's handsome, I was smitten, and I trusted him ... so I followed him
despite my skepticism about veering from the beaten path. The usual
trail we hiked led to a bluff so I wasn't quite sure where this would
go, but I was open. Or so I thought. Sometimes when we keep going
despite feeling the most lost, we find something better than we ever
thought possible. Embracing even the most uncertain changes can
often lead to beautiful destinations.

---

**Sometimes when we keep going despite feeling the
most lost, we find something better than we ever
thought possible. Embracing even the most uncertain
changes can often lead to beautiful destinations.**

---

We kept walking and walking and walking. After all that walking,
I found myself very doubtful that we were headed anywhere. The
trail was muddy, partially washed out from the rain, and difficult to
navigate. I couldn't tell if we were headed anywhere worth seeing
and I began to believe we were probably just walking in circles. We
hadn't brought any food or drinks with us and I was beginning to
get hungry. Actually, I was getting "hangry" — that special kind of
grumpy and bitter that happens when you're hungry and emotional

at the same time. I'm not my best when I'm hangry. Our situation on that muddy trail was becoming serious. I can overcome a lot, but hanger … mmm mmm. Nope. That's where I draw the line.

We started arguing and contemplating turning around and going back toward the truck, assuming we could find our way. The journey back seemed like it would take forever but we had no assurance we were headed anywhere. I started really dragging my feet, grumbling, and just really being a spoilsport about the entire thing. That's when it happened. The wooded trail broke into a huge expanse where the entire forest floor was covered, I mean covered, in buttercups. (Side note: The correct term for these beautiful yellow flowers is daffodils. But round these parts, we call 'em "buttercups," mmmkay?) As far as we could see, the ground was a vibrant yellow and the entire space more fragrant than you can imagine. It was, and still is, one of the most beautiful sights I've ever seen.

The amazing thing is that buttercups don't last that long. They typically only bloom for a few weeks before they fade away. Had Seth and I taken that hike at another time, it's almost certain that we wouldn't have seen those flowers in such glory. Had we not continued along the muddy, uncertain path — had we turned back or given into hanger — we would have missed that beautiful, fleeting sight. We would have missed out on it and never had the chance again, at least not that year. The worst part is that if we had turned back, we would have never even known what we missed. We wouldn't have learned a single lesson about resilience or endurance or being open-minded about what lay ahead. We would have kept right along resisting — resisting the mud and the worry and the hunger and the discomfort about not knowing our way — completely ignorant to what God had in store for us.

The same is true for change. The journey is hard. Sometimes it takes way longer than we'd like and sometimes we get completely lost.

The journey is what it's all about. And the lessons are many, if you're willing to learn.

So, Buckle Up, Buttercup ... you're in for quite a ride!

## CHAPTER I

# Choosing the Road Less Traveled

*Seasons come, and seasons go,*
*Winds pulling branches to and fro.*
*The oak, unyielding,*
*Stands strong against the wind.*
*First a snap ... it hits the ground.*
*The wind whistles at the sound.*
*As for me, when I face the wind,*
*I choose instead*
*To bend.*

If you learn nothing else from this book, I hope you learn to bend ... to be less afraid of the wind and of the changing seasons of our lives.

Have you ever heard any of the following statements?

- "I hate change."

- "This wasn't a change we needed. If it's not broken, don't fix it."
- "They don't bother asking before they make these changes."
- "I'm too old to change."
- "No matter how hard I try, I can't change it."
- "It's too late to change this now."

I've heard them all. In fact, I've *made* some of those statements before (maybe all of them!). "Change" is one of those words that generates a mix of emotions for those who hear it. Some people thrive on change but, for most, change is awkward, uncomfortable, and sometimes downright unpleasant. Sometimes we are faced with changes we didn't ask for and other times we need to make changes that seem impossible. Regardless, learning to navigate and — dare I say *embrace* — change is a skill and a habit you can leverage in crafting the life you want.

# WHEN LIFE THROWS US CURVEBALLS

Have you ever had to change something you didn't ask for? Maybe it was a necessary change in eating habits due to a diagnosis of high cholesterol, an organizational change that affected your job, a big geographic move, or any number of curveballs life likes to throw our way. How did that feel? Were you open and excited or nervous and resistant? Maybe you were just resigned and somewhat indifferent, which isn't an awful place to be. The mere fact that you've picked up this book might indicate that change isn't your favorite subject and that's okay! Regardless of how easy-going you are in the best of circumstances, setting your sights on a difficult change is daunting.

In my late 20s, I found myself smack in the middle of a very unexpected change. I had finished college and was now in the career of my choosing. As an elementary school teacher, I thought I'd be doing what I loved, but I was miserable! I had simply made the wrong choice. *Big* wrong choice. I felt discouraged, unfulfilled, and stressed every day. I knew, early on, that being a teacher, at least in this way, wasn't the career for me, but I stayed. I stayed for six years in something that didn't bring me joy.

Now, don't get me wrong. I don't believe in being blissed-out every second of the day. Life is filled with challenges and obstacles that require grit and determination to get through. Everyone has hard days at work, and I realize that work is, well, *work*. Just because something is hard doesn't mean it's worth giving up on. In this situation, though, I knew in my heart that it wasn't getting better. I knew I had made the wrong choice for myself. And I knew that no amount of grit or determination would change that. So I chose, finally, to hang up my lesson plans, smiley faces, flashcards, and all those silly standardized tests and become a corporate trainer. I'm so glad I did.

We are faced with countless choices each day. It's been estimated that the average adult makes approximately 35,000 choices every day.[1] It's no wonder that our brains shift to autopilot and handle some of those choices for us to prevent complete exhaustion. Out of 35,000 choices, do you know how many it takes to completely alter your course? One. It takes only one choice to make an everlasting impact on the course of your life. In my case, I had been on autopilot for too long. I was making choice after choice without consideration or intention. That path had led me to a career with which I was completely unhappy. But this career crisis didn't just happen to me; it had been a choice all along. And during the six years when I hated my job but stayed, that had been a choice too — a choice to resist change and accept misery instead.

---

1    Eva M. Krockow, PhD. "How Many Decisions Do We Make Each Day?" PsychologyToday.com. *Psychology Today*, Sep. 27, 2018.

Ask yourself: What are your goals in life? Where do you want to be and what are you doing to get there? If you know what you want out of this thing called life, and you know the steps you need to take to get it, then you must ask yourself: What exactly is holding you back? There are so many things that hold us back from pursuing the lives we really want. Maybe you're worried about what others think of you. Maybe other obligations take up all your time. Maybe you lack support from friends or family. Maybe you're scared of failing. Recognize now that — regardless of what it is that's holding you back or how insurmountable the obstacles may seem — *you* are *choosing* to let it hold you back. Every day that you let the *thing* get in the way of your *goal*, you are making a conscious choice to settle for less than you deserve or desire.

---

Recognize now that — regardless of what it is that's holding you back or how insurmountable the obstacles may seem — you are choosing to let it hold you back. Every day that you let the thing get in the way of your goal, you are making a conscious choice to settle for less than you deserve or desire.

---

It isn't just "happening" to you. You always have options, even when the situation you find yourself in wasn't your choice. How you react to a situation or get yourself out of it *is* your choice. Maybe your choice is passive, like mine was. Showing up every day to a job I didn't love was a choice to do nothing ... to avoid change. I didn't have a good excuse for staying in my rut, and I just needed to acknowledge it and get going! Maybe your excuse for accepting the status quo or your current situation is valid; perhaps you're a single parent with minimal time and very low income, so your options seem limited. Regardless of your situation, change is a *choice*. You can choose to get started, to raise your hand and express what you're really feeling, to do the work, and get closer to your goals than you were before. Or you can choose to resist change and stay right where you are. Big transformations in our lives and careers don't always take place overnight, and you might need to get creative to craft the future that you seek, but the choice is all yours. Meaningful change hinges on *choice*.

# THERE WILL ALWAYS BE BACKSEAT DRIVERS

By now, you've surely noticed my repeated use of a "journey and driving" metaphor to help us think about and tackle the concept of change. I think the metaphor is apt because creating or embracing change is about forward motion, while resisting it is about applying the brakes or making U-turns. So, in the pages ahead, you'll hear me talk about everything from steering wheels and seat belts to pit stops and carpooling. I think you'll find the analogy helpful in teaching and inspiring you to move more efficiently through your personal and professional lives.

So let's talk for a minute about backseat drivers. If you have a goal, you have the desire to change. Period. It is impossible to grow and succeed without changing along the way. Change is an inevitable and beautiful process. But change is also *hard*. It is hard for a variety of reasons, but most of those reasons center around fear. We develop fears for all sorts of reasons and have many real experiences that might explain why we have developed those fears. One of the most common fears that holds people back from making positive change is the fear of what others will think. It certainly played a part in why I hadn't started pursuing my goal of becoming a published author until recently. I was afraid people would think I was egotistical for embarking on such a goal. I was afraid others would think I was uppity and full of myself. I held off working toward a dream because I was scared. Friends, there will *always* be naysayers or judges — people I call backseat drivers. If a fear of what others think is something you struggle with, you most likely have a backseat driver story of your own.

---

**One of the most common fears that holds people back from making positive change is the fear of what others will think.**

---

The first backseat driver I remember encountering was a middle school teacher of mine, Mr. Shriner. He taught a "career studies" class that I suspect was one of those courses created to meet some need that had arisen by changes from the state education department. As such, there were likely no teachers at my school with deep expertise in career studies or even a whole lot of passion on the topic. I'm guessing Mr. Shriner was given a curriculum and told "good luck." This suspicion helps me try to understand his perspective in the story where he's clearly the antagonist. You see, most backseat drivers operate from a place of unhappiness in their own lives. Such an environment was undoubtedly fueling Mr. Shriner's negativity. Perhaps I was doomed from the start.

Into my career studies class I walked, knobby kneed and ready to take on the world. I was young but I had career aspirations already. I had always aspired to act, write, speak and lift others up by helping them find their strengths. I was just outgoing and tenacious enough to make myself known and hadn't yet considered the possibility that others wouldn't see things the way I saw them. On our first day of class, we were given the assignment to write one paragraph about what we wanted to be when we grew up and why. I was filled with excitement. I genuinely remember being so thrilled to explore my dreams on paper and to get feedback from someone who clearly had all the answers. After all, one doesn't get placed in charge of students' career paths haphazardly, right? I was ready to look up to Mr. Shriner and to share my dreams.

---

**I had always aspired to act, write, speak and lift others up by helping them find their strengths.**

---

Eagerly, I wrote a strong and convincing paragraph about my desire to act, write, and speak for people. I wrote about wanting to inspire others and to make them laugh. I wrote about my general zest for helping others. I included evidence from plays I had been in, speeches I had given, and even shared my success in portraying "Mrs. Manners" for my elementary school's morning news report. I really thought it through and put in as much passion as my tween self could muster. I handed my paragraph in with a smile and waited silently for my turn with Mr. Shriner.

He was calling up each student individually. I was about to burst with excitement and could barely sit still. I assumed he was exploring ways in which we could turn our aspirations into action and how, even as pre-teens, we could begin molding our futures to match our dreams. I couldn't wait to learn exactly what my journey would look like to achieve my dreams. I just *knew* I was about to receive valuable advice on exactly what I needed to do to make everything a reality.

I watched each friend pass by Mr. Shriner's desk, and I eagerly awaited my turn. Surely, he would confirm my aspirations. Every teacher I had up to this point had given me nothing but encouragement toward the same goals. It had been written on report cards and parent notes and scribbled into my yearbook many years already. Everyone knew I was going to be an actress, a writer and a professional speaker. Mr. Shriner was sure to agree that this was the path for me. Spoiler alert, but in the history of bubbles, I don't think anyone has formed a bigger and more easily burst bubble than I had in that moment. Finally, my turn came, and I did a little skip-walk up to his desk. Flashing my usual ear-to-ear grin, I eagerly awaited his words of wisdom that would propel me into my bright and shining future. What happened next was not at all what I expected.

Mr. Shriner said something to me that I won't forget as long as I live. "Look, there are enough actresses out there and everyone wants to do stuff like write books or help people. You need to choose something you can do that we *need* in society. You need to choose something realistic. What you need to consider are attainable careers, like being a truck driver."

Now, the joke was on him, because driving would never be a strong suit of mine. My parallel parking skills usually make anyone near me laugh hysterically and I have had to ask for help backing out of a tight spot more times than I care to admit. (Don't let the "buckle up" theme of this book fool you. I don't have what it takes to be a professional driver!) As funny as it is now, at that age, this advice from my teacher really discouraged me. Being a truck driver didn't appeal to my interests in the least and, I assure you, my lack of hand-eye coordination was evident at a very young age. I was completely deflated. It was like someone had told me that all my strengths were for nothing. I felt like he was telling me that the few gifts I had been given were of no use to the world.

As an adult, I can look back on Mr. Shriner's words and understand where they came from. But as a child, they stung. It took me a long time to realize that his words reflected his own life experiences and weren't a personal assessment of my character or skills. He was probably a pragmatic guy whose passions had been stifled and he might have been a teacher who hated teaching (as would, ironically, be the case for me in another decade). What I did learn from this heartbreaking experience is that there are *always* backseat drivers in our lives. Backseat drivers are people who will always discourage you, critique you, judge you, second-guess you, and ultimately fill you with doubt and steer you away from the lane where you were meant to drive. The trick is to remember that we are in the driver's seat, and that backseat drivers are welcome to their opinions but they have no control over the pedals or the wheel. I'm convinced that, in our careers and in our personal lives, most backseat drivers mean well and want to advise us away from potential disappointment or bad experiences they've had in their own lives. Nine times out of 10, though, we let those negative individuals get in our heads and hold us back.

So what can you do if backseat drivers affect *your* road trip?

## CHOOSE TO TAKE THE WHEEL

We live in an era of social media, with memes for every situation, viral videos and entire movements on "being yourself" or "embracing your dreams," yet we all still seem to struggle with choosing to do what makes us better. We let backseat drivers and the opinions of others hold us back.

I suspect that everyone can readily identify someone in their life who they would call a backseat driver. Who were or are *your* backseat drivers? When we first think about these naysayers, it may seem like these folks have control of the wheel but, from now on, I'd like to challenge you to change your perspective. Instead of taking the opinions of others (or even your own initial perceptions of a situation) at face value or as cardinal truth, try shifting your perspective instead.

Let me share another childhood story. And, no, it's not about corn worms! I started the 6th grade in a brand-new town. My parents had decided to move and were building a house about 30 miles from where I had grown up. I had gone from attending an elementary school ("my" elementary school, as far as I was concerned) with friends I had made for years in a very diverse community to suddenly attending a school in a rural community with a very different social landscape. When I started middle school, I was terrified. Suddenly, I found myself surrounded by peers who had no clue who I was and who didn't know anything about me. I went from being extremely outgoing to extremely reserved ... really fast. Because I felt uncomfortable, I started to find several reasons *not* to accept the change. I resisted the opportunities of my new community and my new school, believing instead that being the "new kid" was the worst thing in the world. I told myself that the kids were mean, cliquey, and not as good as the friends I left behind. I found ample reasons to isolate myself and not participate in extracurricular activities. I would come home from school and pick up the phone to call one of my former friends and complain for hours about having to live in a new place.

Eventually, my former friends moved on. They were involved in school activities and stopped answering the phone when I called ... probably because nobody likes to listen to someone only sharing negativity. With no former friends and no new friends, I turned to pleading with my parents to move back. My mother, likely at her wit's end, finally had a much-needed conversation with me about change. In the South, we call this a "come-to-Jesus" talk. She held me accountable for my feelings by pointing out that the way I was viewing things was all wrong. How I was seeing the situation was impacting my behavior and, therefore, affecting how I was being received by my peers.

Keep in mind that, at 12 years old, I thought my mom's assessment was complete nonsense. But I have always been a firm believer in "don't knock it 'til you've tried it." And because I was already so miserable, I figured that taking my mother's advice couldn't possibly make it any worse. Right? So, I decided to change how I was seeing the situation. Instead of thinking about how much I missed my old friends, I decided to focus on the opportunity to make new friends. Instead of focusing my time on trying to reconnect with kids in my previous hometown, I started getting out of my comfort zone and reaching out to kids in my new town. It turned out that they weren't so bad after all! They weren't mean, cliquey, or trying to leave me out. They had simply been responding to what I had been putting out there. When I was sad and resistant, they weren't likely to extend themselves in friendship. But once I became friendly and optimistic, I became someone they wanted to know.

This was the first time in my life I can remember understanding that my thoughts (and how I viewed entire situations) was completely my own choice. Did I have control over my parents choosing to move? No. Did I have control over the location they selected? No. Did I have control over my former friends moving on with their lives? No. I *did*, however, have control over whether I let those things effect my mood or my behaviors. That, my friends, is what choosing to take the wheel is all about. Letting a backseat driver take control is a choice. In this situation, I had been my own backseat driver, letting pessimism and victimization steer my course. But when I buckled up to drive my own success, everything changed.

Ask yourself: Do you have a backseat driver in your life? Maybe *you* are your own backseat driver. Have you reacted to the words of such naysayers (or your inner dialogue) and soaked up that negativity like a sponge? Do you soak in everything they say and mull over it for days? Are you facing an unwelcome or difficult change that you have let permeate your mood and, therefore, your relationships? Do these responses affect how you live your life?

Take a huge step in the right direction today by recognizing that how we respond to backseat drivers is a *choice* and that we have other options. Tomorrow, react to their words like a mirror. Reflect their words back to them, helping them understand what you hear them saying but refusing to let them dull your shine.

Instead of resisting change and viewing it as a negative path, I encourage you to consider that backseat drivers can actually be helpful. Consider their cautions and complaints as fuel in your endeavors. Be grateful that whatever you're doing is worth the chatter. You can't control what others say but you *can* control how you receive it. Remember, recognizing that we have *choice* is the first step in making positive changes and accepting changes we didn't have control over.

---

Recognizing that we have choice is the first step in making positive changes and accepting changes we didn't have control over.

---

# GRAB HOLD OF THE WHEEL

*Welcome to the interactive portion of this book-reading experience: Pit stops! You'll find "pit stops" at the end of each chapter. Like any pit stop, these exercises are meant to be an opportunity to refresh and replenish, with activities that make you think about and take action to help you reach your destination.*

*Reflecting on your goals and choices, answer the following questions.*

**What changes are you currently facing?**

_____

_____

_____

_____

**What factors are holding you back from embracing the changes you need to make?**

_____

_____

_____

_____

**What choices can you make today to move forward with courage?**

_____

_____

_____

_____

## CHAPTER 2

# Comparison Causes Traffic Jams

*I glanced at you ...*
*What did I see?*
*Everything that was wrong with ME.*
*I looked closer ...*
*What did I do?*
*Remembered you had wrong things TOO.*
*You are you,*
*And I am me ...*
*Exactly what we're meant to BE.*

We know that there will always be backseat drivers in everything that we do, especially when it comes to changing, growing and bettering ourselves. Backseat drivers everywhere! We find them at work, church, in our friend groups and even in our family. But what happens when the backseat driver lives inside your own mind? How do we overcome being our own biggest naysayer? In this chapter, we are going to learn how to stop that cycle of thought, surround ourselves with people and things that feed our mind with encouraging thoughts, and talk about behaviors that strengthen our inner cheerleader!

Let me tell you a quick tale of a group of individuals — all aged twenty-something — who we will lovingly refer to as the Rat Racers. To set the stage, the Rat Racers grew up together in privilege. They all came from families who told them they were special no matter what, and they had parents and grandparents who always gave them what they wanted. They each received a college education that was paid for by their parents or they fearlessly racked up student loan debt with complete assurance that they'd get an awesome job and pay it off quickly. Collectively, their biggest aspirations are to be the big fish in the small pond of a town where they grew up. Now they're all adults and they're all in competition with each other. In the Rat Racer social circle, it's all about how everything *looks*. Each young man or woman is trying to buy the nicest house on the better lot in the "it" neighborhood. They are trying to have the *best* wedding, the *best* car, and the *best* job. And they all use social media to prove just how amazing their lives really are. They're all best friends (sort of) until one of them has success and the competition heats up again. As Dave Ramsey would say, "We buy things we don't need with money we don't have to impress people we don't like."1 Sound familiar? I'm willing to bet that wherever you are, you have either witnessed or participated in the rat race.

---

1    Dave Ramsey, *The Total Money Makeover: A Proven Plan for Financial Fitness,* Thomas Nelson, 2003.

# APPEARANCES AND COMPARISONS

In the social media age, it's incredibly hard not to compare your journey to others. Every day, people are posting the best versions of themselves to social media. As I write this, I can't help but think back to family pictures we recently took. Every single photo that I posted online was truly picture perfect. I didn't share the "outtakes" and, in fact, the photographer never showed me the dozens or hundreds of shots that were duds. The photographer who worked with us did an amazing job of capturing every smile, hug, kiss, and happy moment. What you *won't* see when you look at my post is that it was 95 degrees outside, we were sweating, the kids were cranky, there was fussing and pouting, and everything was far from perfect. And while it's okay to share our favorite images or most pride-worthy stories, it's important to remember that what we see and share online is inevitably polished or curated with a specific reaction in mind.

When you're looking at posts from your peers on Facebook or Twitter, LinkedIn or Instagram, you don't usually get to see the ugly. You don't see the blood, sweat, and tears that went into what they "have." You don't see their absentee parent or their unhappy marriage. You don't get to see someone struggling with addiction, anxiety, or feelings of hopelessness. You don't see the financial debt or the career burnout or the 20 pounds they've recently gained. You're only seeing the best version *and* you're only seeing what they want you to see. This has created a misleading and sometimes toxic place of comparison within our minds; this "comparison culture" can be hard to overcome.

The backseat driver in your mind will tell you that your friend's promotion means that you're less successful. You'll see that new car someone got and it will make you appreciate your perfectly roadworthy car less. The backseat driver inside of you will compare your reality to the façade of others and make you feel "less than." It will make you chase after things that don't matter and pull you off the path to achieving your goals and focusing on what is truly important to you. Comparison will steer you completely off course and prevent you from leveraging what you're facing for the better. Whether you are trying to deal with change you don't have control over *or* you're trying to create positive change in your own life, comparison will derail the process.

---

The backseat driver in your mind will tell you that your friend's promotion means that you're less successful. You'll see that new car someone got and it will make you appreciate your perfectly roadworthy car less. The backseat driver inside of you will compare your reality to the façade of others and make you feel "less than."

---

Let's look at a few ways you can say goodbye to the rat race and kick comparison to the curb!

# KICKING COMPARISONS TO THE CURB

## Comparison Exercise A:
## Pump the Social Media Brakes

If managing your social media interactions is dragging you down, you have two options. You can get off social media completely *or* you can make friends with the unfollow, unfriend, and block buttons! You have complete control over the content you view on social media and you can curate the incoming content to motivate and inspire you to reach your goals. If your goal is to get fit, then you need to unfollow anyone who isn't supportive of that lifestyle. Follow people and groups who post fitness tips and motivational words.

When you've spent time comparing your reality to the image others carefully curate, it is extremely freeing to unfollow and no longer see anything that gives you anxiety. It sounds like a no-brainer to be proactive about reducing stress from social media, but social media becomes a habit. What we see on social media affects our thoughts, our thoughts affect our behaviors, and our behaviors effect our success (or lack thereof). Everything you view on social media should be something that motivates you and makes you better.

---

## What we see on social media affects our thoughts, our thoughts affect our behaviors, and our behaviors effect our success (or lack thereof).

---

Sometimes the answer may be getting rid of social media altogether, or at least some forms of it. Take inventory of the digital and social media you are consuming. Take time to write down and figure out what your digital habits are. I love that our phones now tell us what our screen time is and how we spend it. What a kick in the pants! A friend and I were recently laughing because she shared with me that she felt so accomplished at having limited her Facebook time ... until her phone let her know that she had recently spent four hours on Instagram looking at home décor photos! We laughed, but even home décor photos can become toxic if they are making you feel like your home and belongings aren't good enough.

Have you ever heard nutritionists talk about *adding* healthy foods into your diet instead of *eliminating* bad foods from it? I look at social media the same way. If you have developed a habit of waking up and immediately checking social media, offer yourself a healthy replacement. If you're seeking to make positive changes and grow yourself, this is an excellent way to take advantage of pockets of time that may not be serving you otherwise. For example, I recently recognized that, on many mornings, one of the first things I was doing was grabbing my phone and checking social media. That small, often mindless practice was doing nothing to help me achieve my goals or to get my day started on a positive note. Instead of deleting social media apps I downloaded an app that serves up articles based on my interests and some books I had been looking forward to reading. Now, when I grab my phone in the mornings, I go to those apps first, take advantage of the early morning time to read, learn, and grow. It has made all the difference in how my day transpires and it sets me up for success. I encourage you, while seeking or navigating change, to take inventory of your social media habits and leverage those practices to your advantage.

**Go ahead and try it. Make a list of apps to add to your phone or steps in your routine that will help you lessen your focus on unhealthy comparisons.**

_____

_____

_____

_____

**Now list the people, groups, or pages you can unfollow to ensure that you're only viewing content that truly serves, motivates, educates, or inspires you.**

_____

_____

_____

_____

# Comparison Exercise B:
# Circle of Friends

We've already talked about how negative folks can show up anywhere. It could be a coworker, a family member, or even a lifelong friend. Remember, change is _hard_. If you're dealing with an organizational change that you can't control, there's a good chance someone negative may not be on board with the change and doesn't want you to be on board with it either. The same can be said if you are seeking to make positive changes in your own life. My first suggestion about what to do if you encounter a negative person in your circle of friends is to no longer spend time or energy on that person. However, sometimes they are a family member or someone you've known for a very long time. In this case, you might not want to completely disassociate with them. Much like we discussed before, instead of eliminating, seek to *add* positive friends to your circle!

Let's take a minute and learn how to identify positive people. It seems silly, but when you are surrounded by backseat drivers, it might not be easy to recognize a positive person. Yet they should be on the top of your list of people to add to your circle. Positive people accept change. In fact, they often *seek out* ways to change and grow (e.g., they're always signing up for webinars and workshops, they're considering going back to school for a graduate degree, they're the first to volunteer for a committee or an assignment, they're always redecorating their house, or they're trying out new restaurants and yoga studios). These change-embracers see organizational change as a catalyst for professional growth and always look for opportunity in challenging situations. They are the people in the break room reading books instead of stirring pots. They are the enterprising team members who pave their own way and don't get easily ruffled.

When it comes to creating positive change, they are experts. They face challenging situations with courage and are ready to roll up their sleeves and work hard to create the lives they want. They never let fear hold them back and they always try to learn from their mistakes. Depending on your situation, you may not have a positive person in your current circle. If not, get out of your comfort zone and go find them. Consider joining a professional organization of like-minded people and look for church or social groups that bring positive people into your circle. Is there someone in your office you haven't gotten to know because they aren't participating in the office chatter? Perhaps there is a member of your leadership team that you'd love to have as a mentor but have been too withdrawn to ask. Be brave! Whatever you need to do, seek out positive individuals who will support and encourage the change you're working toward.

One of the biggest perspective changes regarding friends and who you surround yourself with happened when I was in high school. My freshman year of high school, I discovered what it meant to have a frenemy — a friend who is at least partially, if not entirely, a true enemy. She was someone I had grown up with, trusted, and loved dearly, but it turned out that she spent most days telling me all the negative things other people supposedly said about me. She never would point out exactly who said what, but would simply let me know that "someone" in "some class" didn't like my shirt, or personality, or shoes, or ... you get the idea. I really took her "friendly advice" to heart. After all, she was my friend. I'd agonize and bemoan to my parents about all the troubling news my dear friend was uncovering about me.

Eventually, my mother, who had heard enough, started asking me a few more questions about my woes and put two and two together. My mother then told me that "What your friend is saying about you says more about her than it does about you." Up until that point, I had only seen her as a good friend. In fact, I defended her to my mom and assured my mom that she was just trying to keep me informed on what everyone else was saying. As it turns out, my mom was right. Aren't they always? My friend was really an enemy — a rival, a judge, and a backseat driver.

It was then that the importance of surrounding myself with the right people rang so true to me. I had absolutely agonized over something that was nothing more than classic cattiness. Fortunately, I had no shortage of other amazing friends in high school — many of whom are still supporting, encouraging, and challenging me in the best ways, years later. Instead of letting the backseat drivers take the wheel, I chose to focus on the positive people, and it made all the difference. Evaluate your circle and only invest your energy in people who help make you better.

---

Instead of letting the backseat drivers take the wheel, I chose to focus on the positive people, and it made all the difference. Evaluate you circle and only invest your energy in people who help make you better.

---

**In your personal or professional life, who can and should you partially or completely disassociate from?**

_____

_____

_____

_____

**Where are the truly positive people in your life. Jot down a few names of people who have uplifting personalities and are encouraging, then think about how to invest in relationships with them.**

_____

_____

_____

_____

# Comparison Exercise C: Courage and Conviction

Change is hard for so many reasons. Change that is worth pursuing or enduring takes us out of our comfort zone and makes us better. But embracing change and creating change for yourself is *not* the norm. Most people resist change at all levels. It is my hope that this book will equip you to handle whatever changes you are facing. Maybe you work for an organization that is changing its processes and those changes will affect how you do your job. Maybe you are trying to quit smoking. Maybe you are working to achieve a lifelong goal, like writing a book or getting fit or achieving a professional certification. Whatever journey lies ahead of you, courage and conviction must go along for the ride. You will draw from them constantly and they will make the entire trip easier. Let's take a closer look at each.

## COURAGE

Courage is often defined as being afraid yet doing something anyway. I couldn't agree more. Courage *doesn't* mean there is an absence of fear. Instead, it means you acknowledge the fear but don't let it stop you. It means not being able to see where the road is headed but moving forward regardless. When dealing with change, I want you to think of courage as a muscle. Anytime you are working to build muscle, you exercise, create small tears in the muscle fiber, and are sore for a while as your muscle rebuilds. Over time, the muscle grows and what was once difficult is now easy. Courage is the same way. It must be practiced and exercised. Facing your fears is never easy, sometimes it even physically hurts (like if your goal is to become a bodybuilder!), but we *always* grow when we behave from a place of courage.

My oldest son, Cole, is a golfer. I am not, but watching him has given me an extreme appreciation for this difficult game. Every other week, I go with my son to his golf lessons in a neighboring town. During each lesson, the coach makes tiny tweaks and adjustments that challenge my son to break bad habits and build good ones. Often, these tweaks and adjustments mean that my son will struggle and play poorly as he's learning a new skill. One evening, his instructor, Coach Nathan, said something that has stuck with me on my own journey. At a practice like any other, Nathan made a small adjustment to my son's swing that felt new and awkward and caused him to work muscles he had never worked before. My son became very frustrated and wanted to give up. In this moment, Nathan knelt and said, "The only way to get *more* comfortable is to keep doing what makes you *uncomfortable.*" That, my friends, is the essence of courage. To navigate change, you must flex your courage muscle and keep going when the road gets rough.

## CONVICTION

Courage is a lot harder to exercise if you don't have conviction. Conviction is the *why* behind what drives you. Conviction is what makes the road worth traveling. Convictions develop from our beliefs, values, and that inner fiber that makes us who we are. Maybe you're driven in your work to earn a college degree while working full time because of your conviction to be a good role model to your children.

I like to think of conviction as your reason for deciding to embrace or seek change. It must be bigger than the obvious. For example, if you're changing because your company has told you to, then you need a bigger reason. Maybe the reason is that you want to eventually work in management and this will show your leaders that you are ready. That is conviction to grow and succeed.

All change journeys — no matter how big or small, personal or professional — can benefit from a commitment to your convictions. Perhaps you want your children or family to be inspired by your accomplishments and learn the value of hard work. Perhaps you have a personal health or fitness goal tied to your desire to be the best version of yourself for those who you love. Whatever your reason, your level of conviction is what will drive you to push beyond your limits, reach beyond your comfort zone, and keep going. Conversely, if you don't have a strong conviction, you are less likely to push forward. Your conviction, or your *why,* should be something powerful and meaningful to you. It needs to be something more powerful than any fear you have.

Your conviction must be more powerful than:

- Other people's thoughts and opinions (i.e., backseat drivers)
- Your schedule
- Your energy levels
- The naysayer in your head (i.e., your inner backseat driver)
- Any other potential obstacles that might stand in the way.

My convictions behind writing this book go beyond wanting to become a published author. Instead, my conviction rests in the desire to take lessons I have learned (mostly the hard way) and share them with others who need them. Your conviction must be bigger than the obvious. If your conviction is strong, and you're willing to flex your courage muscle, nothing will stop you. Comparisons won't hold you back and whatever change you are facing will be easier for it!

# COMPARISON CONTRACT

Complete the following worksheet to make a "contract" with yourself regarding how you plan to kick unproductive comparisons to the curb.

| Person(s) You Are Comparing Yourself to and Why | How Are You Interacting with Their Behavior (Social Media, Work, Friend Group, etc.) | What Steps You Will Take to Remove the Temptation to Compare from Your Life |
|---|---|---|
| E.g., Sally Somebody, because she always posts photos of her expensive lifestyle, which makes you feel envious. | Her posts show up in my social media feed and I read them and often hit a "like" or "love" or "wow" button. | 1. Unfollow her on social media<br><br>2. Make a list of things I am grateful for in my own life |
| | | |
| | | |
| | | |
| | | |

## CHAPTER 3

# Roll the Window Down for a Fresh Perspective

*He said, She said,*
*I said too.*
*He can't, She can't,*
*So can't you.*
*He did, She did,*
*Why didn't I?*
*How did all that time go by?*

If you've been reading this book from the beginning, you've surely gathered by now that more than half the battle — when it comes to navigating and embracing change — is about getting in the right mindset. I truly believe that by changing your mind, you can change your life. Navigating change successfully means shifting your perception and viewing change as an opportunity rather than an obstacle. When we find ourselves feeling super resistant or stuck in a predictable rut, our own mindset may be a backseat driver, those dreaded naysayers.

---

## I truly believe that by changing your mind, you can change your life.

---

But I realize it's not always easy to be optimistic, courageous, or full of conviction. Let's be real ... it's not like you can flip a switch and suddenly go from being a change-avoider to being a world-class change-embracer. If you could, I'm betting you would! Working on a positive mindset doesn't mean that everything is all rainbows and unicorns. It doesn't mean we won't feel disappointed, angry, or sad. We all have bad days but, generally speaking, making the effort to keep a positive outlook during times of change can and will make the journey easier for everyone. I like to refer to this positive outlook as the cheerleader mindset.

How did I develop the cheerleader mindset? By being an *actual* cheerleader! It all started when I tried out for basketball in the 7th grade. Before you hear this story, you should know that my athletic abilities have always been lacking. Before I was 10, I had broken both of my arms ... twice. I've always been awkward and clumsy, which is why it surprised several people when I decided to try out for the middle school basketball team. A few friends of mine were trying out for the team, and I decided to go with them. It was common knowledge that everyone made the team but if your on-court performance stank, you may just have to sit the bench. I'm not sure that, at that point, anyone who tried out had ever been cut from the middle school girls' basketball team.

# THERE'S A FIRST TIME FOR EVERYTHING

No doubt, the athletic prowess necessary for basketball was not something I had prepared for. Truth be told, up until the day of try-outs, I hadn't even dribbled a ball. We went through all kinds of drills that day. We ran up and back, and up and back, down the court. Over and over and over … well, you get the picture. We were meant to run while dribbling the ball between and under our legs. It was nothing like normal walking or running, and it was a change in gait that my body wasn't ready for at all. My performance was less than convincing. I really sucked. But I wasn't worried because everyone made the team. Right?

The basketball coach at the time, Mrs. Griggs, was (and still is) one of my favorite teachers of all time. She was kind, an amazing teacher, and had a no-nonsense approach to everything. Still, it came as a surprise when she leaned down to me and said to me, using my maiden name as a term of endearment: "Solly, I'm not putting you on the team. You need to stick with cheerleading."

Now, before you gasp and take that as an insult, let me reassure you that she did me a favor and meant no insult to cheerleaders. It was simply true that my performance was awful. In fact, the next week, during Mrs. Griggs' Advanced Computers Class, I was dribbling the basketball she kept in the classroom and it flew up and hit me right in the face. (To which she replied, "And *that* is why I didn't put you on the basketball team.") I'm sure she saved me a lot of grief and maybe even a few stitches. She also taught me a thing or two about the value of honesty.

# BEING A CHEERLEADER

Long story short, I did follow her advice and stuck with cheerleading. Anyone who knows me knows that cheerleading fits my bubbly, "go team!" personality. It also helped me work on my coordination and awkwardness.

Was I a good cheerleader? No. Did I learn how to do front flips and back flips? No. Did I learn how to fly or jump the highest and stick poses without looking awkward? No. As was the case with basketball, I wasn't very good at the athletic side of cheerleading. Turns out that clumsiness thing tends to follow you. But cheerleaders, despite being athletes in their own right, serve another purpose I was able to embrace. They support the team and energize the crowd. And I could do that.

While I didn't learn to be a backflipping tumbler from my years spent cheerleading, I did learn a great deal. I learned that you can work really hard and still not be the best. I learned that laughing off mistakes was better than pouting about them. Most importantly, I learned that the right words or cheers of encouragement at the right time could light a fire that made the difference between winning and losing.

---

I learned that the right words or cheers of encouragement at the right time could light a fire that made the difference between winning and losing.

---

I learned that the attitude of a single person can ignite an entire team. Your mindset in life is the same way. There will *always* be someone smarter, better, faster, or more qualified than you. There will always be problems and difficulties. The mindset with which you approach any obstacle or change makes all the difference.

As a cheerleader, I was on the sidelines of basketball players and football players (and a whole team of coaches too), who were constantly changing course, adjusting their strategies, throwing the ball a different way, and reacting to one another and their competitors. Those players would face change after change, and it was my job to support them through it — to be the opposite of a "backseat driver" who second-guesses each play or cheers "Boo! You'll never succeed!"

# CHANGE EMBRACER OR CHANGE AVOIDER?

Up to this point in this book, we've talked a lot about the overall challenge and opportunity of approaching change, and we've talked about the people who can steer us off course when we're trying to drive success (i.e., those dreaded backseat drivers). We've also just introduced the antidote for the backseat drivers — the cheerleaders. When you have the opportunity to witness others — at home or at work — going through major changes, I hope you'll choose to be a cheerleader and not a backseat driver. (And I hope you'll resist the urge to be your own backseat driver when you could be your own internal cheerleader.)

So now let's talk about YOU — about the person in the driver's seat and how you can be better buckled up and prepared to drive success by embracing change.

At its simplest definition, there are two kinds of people when it comes to our attitudes about change: change embracers and change avoiders.

Let's compare how they each view change.[1]

| Change Avoiders | Change Embracers |
|---|---|
| View change as unnecessary | Know change is inevitable |
| Avoid change | Embrace change |
| Blame others | Accept responsibility |
| Gossip-talk about people | Discuss concepts and ideas |
| Complain, judge, point out flaws | Distribute praise and offer solutions |
| Operate from feelings and emotion | Operate from values and principles |
| Don't have time | Make time |
| Can't | Can |
| Feel helpless to the situation | Know and weigh all options |
| Are generally pessimistic | Are generally optimistic |
| See change as a problem | See change as an opportunity or, at worst, a cloud with silver linings |
| Feel powerless | Feel empowered |

Whether the change you are experiencing is voluntary or involuntary, how you approach it means everything. Change Avoiders tend to view change as unnecessary. They may say something like "If it ain't broke, don't fix it." On the flip side, Change Embracers know that change is inevitable. Change is a part of life. The process is almost always awkward and uncomfortable, but the result is that we

---

1    Disclaimer: This overview is about your mindset and is an observation based on my experiences dealing with change and helping others to navigate it. I am not a healthcare or mental health professional but I realize that chronic pessimism, unresolved emotion, fear, or feelings of depression may be serious and require attention from a medical professional. If you have feelings of depression, fear, anxiety, despair, anger, or frustration that are interfering with your daily activities and life, please contact your doctor or other medical professional. I am not a doctor or medical professional of any kind. If you have feelings of depression contact a medical professional.

grow and become better than we were before. In an organization, you may initially view an imposed change as unnecessary because you don't have all the information regarding why the change is being made.

In addition to viewing change as unnecessary, Change Avoiders will do precisely what their name implies: they'll avoid change like it's the plague! Change Embracers, on the other hand, will initially or eventually realize that change is inevitable. Change is necessary for survival. This isn't just true for individuals, but it is also true for companies. It's been said of businesses that "If you're not changing, you're dying," and there's a whole lot of truth in that. Everything is in a constant state of flux — technology, the social climate, the actual climate, the economy, consumer expectations, trends. When we avoid change, we hurt ourselves because we actively limit our potential. Change is happening every second of every day — in our personal lives and in our careers — whether we like it or not. Embracing change means that we let go of our fears and are open to grow.

---

## When we avoid change, we hurt ourselves because we actively limit our potential.

---

When it comes to fear, Change Avoiders typically experience a lot of it. Some Change Avoiders are downright overcome or paralyzed by their fears — fear of failure, fear of what others think, and fear of the unknown. One obvious symptom of fear is looking to blame others for your own unhappiness. Change Avoiders tend to get stuck in a negative mindset, then engage in gossip and judge others because they feel helpless. They may say things like "This would be a great place to work if I had an office or a better title" or "I'd like to lose weight but I'm like my Mom, she always had a sweet tooth." They also love nothing more than to point out flaws in others. You may hear things like "Of course she's going to act bubbly ... what else does she have going for her?" or "If I were managing this place, we'd never experience this kind of turnover." Fear is paralyzing. It leaves you feeling stagnant and stuck. If we think back to the Rat Racers, they each held the fear of not looking as good as someone else. Because they had the fear of someone else's success making them appear less successful, they made poor choices that ultimately put them on the wrong paths.

Because Change Embracers, conversely, typically are undaunted by a certain amount of fear, they're more apt to know how to accept responsibility and control their feelings. Change Embracers typically don't waste time talking negatively and spinning their wheels. They are discussing concepts and ideas that will bring them closer to their goals. They praise the success of others and offer solutions instead of judgment. If you've been finding yourself engaging in negative talk, try forcing yourself to speak positively about others; it might feel awkward or inauthentic at first, but I promise it will help change your mindset.

The title of this chapter is "Roll the Window Down for a Fresh Perspective" — and examining new perspectives requires a willing to "just be real." If we are being completely real, we *all* have naysayer moments — moments where even the most practiced Change Embracer starts feeling like an Avoider, maybe even sabotaging themselves with internal backseat driving. It's inevitable that change is going to rattle us or trigger from time to time, especially in the presence of certain situations that cause us to put up protective walls or certain people who bring out fear or defensiveness in us. So being aware of the necessary mindset shift for embracing change isn't always enough — you also need tools!

I call these tools the Three Rs: recognize, rejuvenate, reset.

# RECOGNIZE

Most of us are self-aware enough to notice when we're feeling negative and crummy but it's possible to get into a rut and not even realize it. The first step to turning your attitude around is to *recognize* that you need to. A negative mindset usually reveals itself in the way we talk about others. You can safely say that you're in a negative mindset if:

- You catch yourself speaking poorly about others
- You find yourself passing judgment on others instead of simply observing their behaviors
- You blame other people for your situation, or
- You find yourself avoiding all interaction with others.

---

### A negative mindset usually reveals itself in the way we talk about others.

---

The good news is that *if* you take the time to recognize the state you are in, then you are well on your way to feeling — and behaving — better.

Many changes we encounter — at work and at home — are entirely out of our control but can still shake us to our core. Recognizing that we've encountered something deeply disruptive to our emotions, routines, sense of self, and/or confidence in the future (i.e., we've encountered "change" or the first inklings that change is on the way) is the first step in turning our mindset around.

By way of example, let me share a deeply personal story. Try as we all might, sometimes we fail to recognize our negative mindsets at first and, if we're not working to recognize our feelings, attitudes, words, and behaviors, such negativity can linger for a very long time. It's Mother's Day 2020 as this book receives its final editorial touches before heading off to press, and today my husband and I are celebrating parenthood with our sons — the two sweetest boys you can imagine. But our road to parenthood wasn't easy. We had several miscarriages along the way and, in 2015, we suffered a miscarriage during the second trimester of pregnancy. That pregnancy was much further along than our previous pregnancies and we had a much greater hope for the future than we had felt (or even allowed ourselves) for quite some time. Losing that baby was a huge blow and a change that we had no control over. The loss left a deep sadness that we both still feel.

Months later, I was still feeling like a shell of myself. I was in an extremely negative mindset and it had permeated into everything I was doing. Everything as shadowed by a dark cloud — work, interactions with my family, everyday life. I couldn't see the good in anything. One day, while in the middle of telling a dear friend of mine my laundry list of negativity and grievances, she said something that I will never forget. She said, "I don't want you to take this the wrong way, but I think you're dealing with some postpartum issues." It was like someone had turned on a light in a dark room. I had always heard about baby blues and postpartum issues after having a baby, but I didn't have a baby I could bring home. It had never occurred to me that those same things could happen after miscarriage. Without my sweet friend, I might have never recognized the mindset I was in and I would have never taken the steps I needed to fix it. In my case, addressing my mindset required more than just an attitude adjustment. I had to not only recognize what I was experiencing, but I had to seek the advice of a medical professional on how to navigate through it. Being aware was only the first step on a very long road to recovery and healing.

Are you aware of your current mindset? Even when it's just a little bit negative, mildly bitter, or slightly self-absorbed, that kind of mindset can put you at risk of not seeing opportunities all around you — of not embracing the changes that can drive success in your life and your career. If you endeavor to take time each day to recognize how you're *viewing* the world, you significantly increase the odds that you'll be able to understand what impact that viewpoint has on what you're *doing* in the world (and adjust, if necessary).

# RESET

Once you *recognize* the negative mindset you've adopted, it's time to think about why you're feeling and behaving in this way, and then take some time to *reset* yourself. If I'm feeling particularly nasty, it helps when I write all my thoughts down. I take a sheet of paper and I write down every single thought that comes to mind. Often, there will be to-do items, things bothering me, something someone said, grocery lists ... whatever the thought may be, I put it to paper. If it's occupying my mind, it deserves my deliberate attention. Once I have those thoughts on paper, I sort them into two categories: things I can control and things I can't control. For example:

| Things I Can Control | Things I Can't Control |
|---|---|
| • My reactions to the world around me<br>• Getting kids to t-ball<br>• Sending email reminders to others<br>• Taking time to encourage someone today | • Someone's negative comment<br>• Whether t-ball will be canceled due to rain<br>• Whether someone hasn't finished their project<br>• What other people think of me |

It seems simple but putting your thoughts on paper and sorting them can be profound because it helps you to shift your perspective. You can quickly go from being completely stressed out about whether t-ball practice is going to be canceled to focusing on getting the kids to practice on time, come what may. You can "reset" your focus. This is especially helpful for those pesky thoughts that wake you up in the middle of the night. You know the ones. You're peacefully asleep, then BAM ... it's 2:00 a.m. and you're wondering if you've done enough age-appropriate education to teach your kid about "stranger danger." Anybody else? Just me. Cool.

Having command of your thoughts is *so* powerful. Capturing them, recognizing their patterns, and learning to control them makes all the difference in the world! When you practice organizing your thoughts — especially those that once seemed overpowering and unstoppable in your mind — you may find those worries and thoughts suddenly don't seem quite so intimidating. You now have a clear framework for what is worth focusing on and you've made it easier to let go of those other thoughts.

We are given a small and precious amount of time on this Earth. If you're giving any of that time to thoughts that don't serve you, take time to reset and get back to what's important!

We are given a small and precious amount of time on this Earth. If you're giving any of that time to thoughts that don't serve you, take time to reset and get back to what's important!

# REJUVENATE

Now that you've gotten all those thoughts out and put them in their proper place, it's time to REJUVENATE! This final tool in the mindset-shifting, change-embracing toolkit is my favorite because rejuvenation is what really turns that negative mindset around. Everyone is busy, busy, busy. Our to-do's, upcoming appointments, even the relationships we treasure most all demand our time. It's incredibly easy to let all the demands keep us from taking time for ourselves. Flight attendants speak truth when they tell you that you can't help your fellow passenger until you put the oxygen mask on yourself. Likewise, we can't tackle our goals and get in a positive mindset if we haven't taken time for ourselves.

So you must ask yourself: "What is it that makes you feel refreshed?" Maybe you love to hike, go fishing, hang out with friends. Perhaps you need to relax with a long bath, massage, or a nice long nap. Do you have some vacation days you could spare? Take a long weekend away and get out of town! Whatever it is that makes your soul smile … DO IT! Maybe one area of your life needs more rejuvenation than another.

A colleague recently told me that one of the most important things they do personally to remain inspired at work is to get out and attend professional events, conferences, and seminars. Hearing this made me realize that while there are *overarching* needs for self-care and rejuvenation, there are also *specific* areas we may need to focus on from time to time. You may be feeling great at work but struggling when it comes to your social life.

Driving success — in any part of our lives — requires rejuvenation or "regular maintenance." I mean, if you keep driving your car, it will eventually need gas, an oil change, new tires, and a litany of other regular maintenance. The different areas of your life are much the same in their need for attention, maintenance, rejuvenation. Here are a few ideas for how you can rejuvenate in whatever area most needs your attention right now:

| Work | • Attend a conference<br>• Listen to a podcast<br>• Read a business-development book<br>• Shadow someone in leadership<br>• Ask someone to mentor you |
|---|---|
| Home | • Spend 10 minutes decluttering a hot spot<br>• Finish that home-improvement project that's been looming<br>• Light a few candles and put on some music |
| Family | • Get your family outside and do something fun!<br>• Call that family member you haven't spoken to in a while |
| Social | • Use travel time for extended catch-up with friends, including those who live far away<br>• Plan a night out with the "guys" or the "girls"<br>• Do something kind for a friend |
| Spiritual | • Read inspiring literature<br>• Volunteer<br>• Make a donation to your favorite charitable organization |
| Physical | • Go for a walk<br>• Join a community running group<br>• Take a fitness class online or at your local gym |

Change — whether you choose the change or it is thrust upon you — can be draining. Positivity is the goal, but if we have neglected our own thoughts and needs, then we will be forever stuck with a negative mindset. And when we're stuck, we can't embrace change or drive opportunity and success in our lives. When navigating and leveraging change, it is vitally important to remember that you are in charge of your own happiness. You determine whether you are being a Change Embracer or a Change Avoider, and you decide whether you listen to the backseat drivers or the cheerleaders. The choice is yours!

If you find that your mindset isn't where you'd like it to be, then take time today to recognize, reset, and rejuvenate yourself ... and get on the path to positivity!

# THE THREE Rs

## Recognize and Reset

**What's on your mind?**

_____

_____

_____

| Things I Can Control | Things I Can't Control |
| --- | --- |
|  |  |

# Rejuvenate

**List three things you can do this week to rejuvenate yourself.**

1. _____

2. _____

3. _____

## CHAPTER 4

# Making a U-Turn

*Behind door one, there is a road ...*
*Another behind door two.*
*Choose, they said,*
*And get it right ...*
*There's only one for you.*
*I did not like the road I chose*
*And so, I found, instead*
*A window with a lovely view*
*And a way to forge ahead.*

If you've made it this far through our exploration of change and our tips for "buckling up" to drive success in your life and career, it's safe to say that you're either preparing to face a change of some sort, you live a life of seemingly constant change, and/or you want to be a source of support and inspiration to employees or others who struggle with change. Whether you're dealing with change that is intentional (i.e., of your own creation) or if it's something you didn't ask for, you need a map. To figure out where you're going, you must find out where you are and how you got here. It sounds simple, but it can be difficult to take a good, hard look at the choices we've made and how they've turned out. For me, this moment happened in 2013 when I came to the realization that I was in a career that was never going to make me happy. To find out how I ended up miserable and burned out at 26, let's look back at a few choices I made along the way.

# NO GPS

I remember entering high school feeling very filled with possibility. Each year, they had us write what we wanted to be when we grew up, so they could keep track in our file. It was clear from my file that I had no clue, as most teenagers don't. After all, when you're a teenager you've had no real experience in a career to be able to decide whether you like it or not. Babysitting, corn shucking, and odd jobs hadn't taught many of us a whole lot about our career options. My file had everything from being a hairdresser, to a horticulturalist, and finally an art teacher. It was evident in my file that I had let Mr. Shriner and the opinion of everyone around me tangle my aspirations beyond recognition. I had chosen to veer completely away from what I truly loved because I was so concerned with the opinions of those around me. Finally, the time came to begin the process of college enrollment and choosing (and even "declaring") a major.

The college and academic major choice were the first that pointed me in the wrong direction. I'm from a very small town and career options, should you choose to stay, seemed (at the time) somewhat limited. As a woman, I distinctly remember feeling like I had only two options: nursing or teaching. I chose teaching and studied locally at Murray State University for the next four years, completing an undergraduate degree in education. I graduated summa cum laude from the university and had a local job in my sights. Only a few months after graduating, I landed a job teaching first grade at the local primary school in my hometown. If there ever was a handbook for high school to college transition, I had followed it to a T! Everything had worked out exactly as I had planned, and I was ecstatic. I began my teaching career filled with possibility and brimming with ideas of how I would change the world, one student at a time.

---

**I began my teaching career filled with possibility and brimming with ideas of how I would change the world, one student at a time.**

---

I was in for a rude awakening. The ideals I had established in my mind about the creative ways I would be able to help students turned out to be in stark contrast to the reality of the public institution where I worked. Their expectations of me were not what I had imagined. I had gone into education because I loved teaching but, instead, I was given very prescribed content and standards to deliver. Every aspect of the field was micromanaged. The state and federal education guidelines I had to follow weren't concerned with what was best for students or how they learned. Instead, everything was driven by test scores and funding. It was an institution that frowned on innovation and focused on students as scores. For me, the sacrifices of participating in something I disagreed with far outweighed the rewards. In my first year, I knew that this was not the career I had hoped for. I had made a big choice, back when I selected my college major, and I had chosen wrong. I had gone into the career world without a map or a GPS, and I got lost.

To make matters worse, I didn't immediately recognize that my best move would have been to course correct or make a big career U-turn ... now. And doing nothing after that first disappointing year in the classroom was my second big choice that I got wrong. I ignored the gut feeling that something was wrong — that I was in the wrong place, doing the wrong thing, for the wrong stakeholders (cute and deserving though those children were). I chalked it up to first-year nerves. The second and third year, I was distracted raising my first son and tried to make myself believe that what I was feeling was overwhelm. At that time, we had a change in administration so I thought maybe that was the issue. My fourth and fifth years saw the birth of my second son and the beginning of my graduate degree. I continued to convince myself that what I was feeling was a result of juggling too many things. It wasn't until my sixth year teaching elementary school, when my second son was toddling around, that I faced what my gut was telling me. It wasn't nerves or overwhelm at all. I loved teaching but I absolutely hated working in public education.

---

**It wasn't until my sixth year teaching elementary school, when my second son was toddling around, that I faced what my gut was telling me. It wasn't nerves or overwhelm at all. I loved teaching but I absolutely hated working in public education.**

---

Two distinct choices — choosing a college major and then choosing to stay for six years in the wrong job. That was all it took to go from wide-eyed high school grad to burned-out twenty-something public educator. I had chosen a career path when I had no real idea what being a teacher would be like, and I had chosen to ignore my gut when it was telling me I'd made the wrong choice. Now I was faced with my third choice. Do I stay in a career I don't like because it provides security, or do I take a huge leap of faith and leave? I had no clue what to do, but I knew I didn't want to be a part of the public education system anymore.

# MAKING A U-TURN

I needed to make a big change — to slam on the brakes and make a U-turn. My children were still little, and my husband and I immediately discussed the possibility of me staying at home with them if I wanted to. Seth was stably employed and I was lucky enough to have this option for a career break to raise our children. So, I seized the opportunity. I trusted that God had led me to this point, and He would get me through.

That choice led me to the end of one path and the beginning of another. I spent the next three years raising my boys, finishing my graduate degree, and figuring out what I wanted to do with my life. This was the first time I had examined the road I had been traveling and other roads that were available. I learned a great deal, mostly about myself. My husband played the role of both cheerleader and backseat driver at times. He challenged me and gave me support and space to explore by assuming the role of sole financial provider. The journey, while I was grateful for it, wasn't without hardships. No change worth making ever is. It was, however, completely worth it. The time I spent learning who I was and what mattered to me led me to understanding the type of organization I wanted to work for, and the type of work I wanted to do.

---

## The journey, while I was grateful for it, wasn't without hardships.

---

With the fresh discovery that I did love teaching but did not love public education, I made the decision to go back to work for an incredibly generous organization I had worked for during college. The organization operated from the same set of values as I did, and that was important to me. They welcomed me back and allowed me to continue teaching — offering me a position as a corporate trainer. Education in the corporate world allowed me to flex those teaching muscles and my creativity without being micromanaged. It was the perfect fit.

Taking a risk and working through hard times led me to a career that genuinely made me excited to go to work every day. And when I think about the future — future projects and jobs and companies and areas of career focus — I know that I have the tools and the right mindset to tackle whatever big changes might lie ahead.

So how do you change your direction when you aren't headed the right way? Are you willing to make a U-turn in life and in work, regardless of what the backseat drivers or cheerleaders are saying?

When it comes to changing direction, there are three important rules to follow: Check Your Rearview Mirror, Slow Down, and Use a Map.

## CHECK YOUR REARVIEW MIRROR

You can't change the choices you've made in the past. Whatever those may be, and whatever obstacles you face now, know that this life is short and that embracing the changes and obstacles is always more efficient than avoiding them. There may be obstacles in your path that seem impossible. Oddly enough, this book is being released smack in the middle of the COVID-19 pandemic. That is not something I could have even imagined when I began writing. Millions of people are currently without jobs and change has been thrust upon us all in ways we couldn't have conceived before now. Being able to back up and look at how we arrived at this point has been important on a global scale and an individual scale as we all work to repair the unforeseen damage the pandemic has caused. There may be financial obstacles, physical obstacles, or other obligations and responsibilities. You may be facing changes in your life or career that you did not ask for but must find a way through. Whatever is blocking your path, start by looking back and figuring out how you got here.

Checking the rearview mirror and looking at our choices isn't easy, especially if you are someone who struggles with taking accountability. In my case, my "rearview mirror" story not only led me to understanding the decisions that led me to the career I didn't love but also shed light on returning to the organization I had worked for whilst in college. For me, I recognized that my career choices had to be completely in line with my personal values for me to enjoy my career. It wasn't completely about the task or performance aspects of a career but, instead, was more about finding a place where the people and the culture aligned with my values and what was important to me. In public education, I struggled because, at my core, I believe students are so much more than scores and standards. It was difficult for me to push standards and set expectations that I didn't believe in. For me, looking back was an opportunity to not only review the bad choices but the good ones too!

When were the times I really enjoyed my career? I realized that I absolutely loved the act of teaching and helping someone to grow and succeed. I was excited to go to work on days I had the flexibility to get creative and provide solutions for learners who struggled. What things had I once been passionate about that I hadn't explored for some time? The standardization of public education had just not given me enough room to spread those wings on a daily basis. Backing up doesn't only show us where we veered off course, but it can also help us get back on track. It can really help to reposition your thoughts to times you were happy, fulfilled, and felt that you were on the correct path.

Conversely, when you look back and determine what steps led you in the wrong direction, the insights you gain might keep you from making those same mistakes again. For me, not listening to my gut was something I realized never worked out well for me. I gave myself time and space to review my decisions and find patterns in them. Not following my gut was a key pattern in the choices I had made that didn't have the impact I hoped for. I had a gut feeling throughout my undergraduate studies that I was much more interested in learners of all ages than just elementary students. However, that undergraduate program had recently been made extra convenient by online courses and satellite campus options. I chose convenience over my gut and it led me astray.

---

### Not following my gut was a key pattern in the choices I had made that didn't have the impact I hoped for.

---

My newfound belief in "trusting my gut" doesn't mean I will solely rely on my gut instincts to direct my steps, but it does mean that I will weigh my intuition the same as I weigh logic and reason when making any decision or change. This is also one way we can leverage change we've learned from in the past as we pursue future endeavors. Next time you're making a decision relative to a change you're facing, don't forget to back up and use your rearview mirror to reflect on lessons from the past to guide you. My friend Kate says that every time she has decided to shed something big – a client or an entire industry she serves, or a complicated and/or expensive process in her business – she's able to better focus. Less is more for her. When she makes new decisions, she looks in the rearview mirror to remind herself to sharpen, focus, let go – to remind herself that her best decisions have been about letting go, not about saying 'yes' to more distraction.

# SLOW DOWN

I have a confession to make. I have a bit of a lead foot. In my car, and in life, I like to operate from the fast lane. No matter what I'm doing, I tend to always feel a sense of urgency surrounding things. When I make a decision, I am full-speed-ahead getting it finished. This can be a good thing when you want to be on time. However, when navigating change of any sort, it is best to slow down, pay attention to details, and take time to consider all the possibilities. This is especially important when facing organizational changes that are stressful. When we get stressed, we feel hurried, rushed, and unprepared. Choices made when we are operating in the fast lane tend to be poor ones. The last thing you want to do when changing your direction is make another set of poor choices. Take your time!

---

**When navigating change of any sort, it is best to slow down, pay attention to details, and take time to consider all the possibilities.**

---

In order to leverage what you're learning about your decisions (and then apply them for the betterment of your life), you must slow down and give yourself space to evaluate them fully. When I decided to quit my former career, I went on career break to care for my young sons. In doing so, I unknowingly gave myself plenty of space to evaluate and explore my decisions before jumping into my next career change. It wasn't until I had that time that I realized I had never simply sat down and thought about what I wanted, what I was passionate about, what was important to me, and what I ultimately loved to do. All those academic exercises about "what do you want to be when you grow up?" — which my teachers had assigned since I was in elementary school — never translated into true exploration of my options as an adult. I had always thought about careers in terms of what was available and in terms of titles. I knew you could be a teacher, doctor, lawyer, etc., but I never thought about what I loved.

It was when I intentionally slowed down that I realized I love people! I love working with, developing, driving, and leading people. It really didn't matter what the job was, the title, the tasks associated with it. If I could do those things with people, I was good to go. I also realized lots of things I didn't like. For example, I don't like isolation. It made sense that I didn't enjoy staring at the same four walls of a classroom day in and day out. I learned that I don't like being micromanaged. Have you ever seen the documents used to evaluate public school teachers? I expect that one day if you Google "micromanagement," a teacher evaluation document will appear.

Teachers are judged on everything from their tone, their demeanor, positive versus negative comments made, and whether this or that "standard" was visible in this format and blah blah blah. (I had a first-grade student vomit all over my legs and feet once. Instead of being fearful of getting sick, my first thought was not to react or say anything negative for fear of being seen as negative.)

Looking back at scenarios in public education that excited me or brought me down helped me learn so much about myself. All those years had passed, and I had never truly taken the time to find those things out for myself. I had been so busy aiming myself toward a "career" instead of toward an opportunity to do what I loved.

Do you know what you love? Do you know where you thrive and what gets you out of bed in the morning? Do you know what you hate or what drags you down? How could gaining clarity about what drives you, what revs your engine, and what feels like a traffic jam to you help you to make better decisions in your life and career?

Slowing down is about giving yourself the time you deserve. Changing your role, responsibilities, mindset, job, health, etc. all take TIME! So many people like to use the phrase "I do my best work under pressure." I think that should be changed to "I do a lot of work under pressure" instead. Our best work, decisions, and choices come when we've given ourselves the space to consider all options and possibilities. That's when we get creative and come up with even better ideas than we'd originally considered. When changing your direction, slow down and give yourself grace to uncover what is most valuable to you!

Then, and only then, can you focus on where you are headed. The goal is to stop letting life — its changes or its status-quo ruts — happen to us and get back into the driver's seat to make deliberate, thoughtful decisions about where we want to go. I don't promise that it's always smooth when you do the driving — there's a reason I tell you to "buckle up" — but when speeding along the highway of modern life, there's no better place to be than the driver's seat.

# USE A MAP

People who are closest to me are surely laughing about the fact that I have chosen a "driving" theme for this book and that I'm using subtitles like "Use a Map." Because while I have developed a keen sense of "direction" for myself personally and on the career front, the same cannot be said for my actual abilities to navigate while driving my car. I go where Siri or my GPS tells me to go, and it's not uncommon for me to find myself somewhere off the beaten path. Not so long ago, I took a wrong turn on a work-related trip and the road went from highway, to one lane, to gravel and continued way out to the middle of nowhere. Not one to be discouraged, I kept driving until I was around more familiar territory and until my cell signal picked back up. But it was disorienting and uncomfortable to be lost.

I suspect you can relate; it's unsettling to be lost and requires a certain amount of faith and optimism. When we are driving and find ourselves off the beaten path, the sensible thing to do is use a map to navigate yourself in the right direction. Navigating change is no different. When trying to determine the best direction to go (even with big personal decisions or career crossroads), having a map is vitally important. Unfortunately, there aren't maps for every change we may encounter in life.

So what do you do where there isn't a map? You must create one for yourself! Think of your map as a guide and stay true to yourself in the moment of choice. Your map should include a "you are here" statement, which outlines where you currently are. It will also need to have a "destination" to keep the end in mind, but the most important part of your map will be what you put in between the end point and the starting point.

On your map, break the ultimate goal into attainable "destinations," milestones, or landmarks. Each should outline how you will get from one to the next and, ultimately, how they will lead you to your destination. For example, let's say you want to change your direction at work. You're currently in an entry-level position but you'd eventually like a job in management. Stops or mini destinations on your map might include taking on a specific increased responsibility, attending a management conference, completing a work-study assignment, and/or developing a growth plan with your supervisor. Not only does a map keep you accountable, but it also makes it easier to stay true to what's important when you have decisions to make.

The decision to change your direction — in your personal life or in your professional career — is never easy. When you find that a situation you are in is no longer serving you, changing direction may be a necessary step. To make any transition as easy as possible, don't forget to back up, slow down, and use a map to ensure you arrive at your exact destination!

# ROADMAP

**Destination (Goal):**

_____

**What three things must happen to achieve your goal? Think of them as mini destinations on the way to the final goal.**

1. _____

2. _____

3. _____

**Baby Steps – Write down some small actions you can take now.**

_____

_____

_____

_____

## CHAPTER 5

# Refuel Your Confidence

*He thought he couldn't*
*But he tried.*
*There it was, always*
*Inside.*
*A spark, a fire,*
*A guide to inspire.*
*He didn't know*
*But now he sees ...*
*Inside there's everything he needs.*

Confidence. Without question, one of the most important elements of taking any risk or making any worthwhile change is confidence. Most often, people within organizations who are resisting change the most lack the confidence to embrace it. Many people view confidence as something you either have or you don't. Instead, I'd like you to think of confidence as something you can build. Confidence, especially in the workplace, is a muscle we must exercise and flex if we are to become more resilient to change and if we want to eventually be Change Embracers for improved personal and organizational success. Each muscle in the human body has a purpose, they impact our overall health, and if you don't use them, they get smaller and weaker. Likewise, we have different stores of confidence for different needs. Some of us naturally have confidence in certain areas and not others. Certain situations and experiences may deplete confidence we once had and increase our confidence in unexpected ways. For this chapter, I'd like to discuss confidence in the following categories: Physical, Spiritual, Relational, Financial, and Professional.

---

**Without question, one of the most important elements of taking any risk or making any worthwhile change is confidence.**

---

# PHYSICAL CONFIDENCE

Physical confidence includes our confidence as it relates to our physical health, fitness, weight, and appearance. How we feel day to day and how well we are taking care of our physical bodies has a direct impact on what we can give to others. Regarding change, it is much easier to embrace changes we've been dealt if we feel good. Conversely, if we are dealing with physical depletion, encountering unwelcome changes could be just enough to tip us over the edge into overwhelm. When we're dealing with changes that are difficult, we tend to get busy and distracted, and one of the first things we scratch off the list is exercise or physical rejuvenation. And that's the last thing we ought to scratch off the list! Taking some time for exercise, a walk outside, or a simple moment to stretch and reconnect with your body can make a significant difference in your ability to take on the day and tackle the work that change requires. Remember, physical confidence isn't just about fitting into your swimsuit. It's about feeling good because you took some time to show your body some love.

## SPIRITUAL CONFIDENCE

Spiritual confidence includes our mental health, personal belief systems, and values. When was the last time you checked in with yours? This confidence store can have a great impact on all the others. If what you are doing daily conflicts with your personal beliefs and values, it can really take a toll on you. For me, I can tell that I'm low in spiritual confidence when I'm feeling uncertain or doubtful of the direction I'm heading. It can look and feel a lot like self-doubt. When that happens, I try to take the time to read scripture, pray, and touch base with mentors who share my values. Finding a practice rooted in your own personal beliefs is deeply important to how you approach decisions every day. Perhaps it involves meditation, deep breathing, or a check-in with a therapist or close friend. Find out what that practice looks like for you and make time to keep your spiritual confidence stores replenished.

## RELATIONAL CONFIDENCE

Confidence in relationships — including family, friends, organizations, and social groups — is vital. This is a huge one for me. Time spent in fellowship with family and friends deeply nourishes my soul. Even more, relational confidence gives us strength to handle difficult situations with grace. In times of change, evidence of relational confidence being depleted looks like teams that are experiencing conflict, disengagement, and just plain-old drama. It is especially important for us to keep in contact with family, friends, colleagues, and other peers while working through a change personally or as a team. Keeping communication open by continuously checking in with one another keeps relationships healthy.

# FINANCIAL CONFIDENCE

Our financial confidence comes from our ability to provide for ourselves and for others from a monetary standpoint. Sometimes changes and situations outside of our control can rapidly deplete our financial confidence. Job loss, sudden medical needs, unexpected expenses (like home or car repairs), or accumulating debt can all take a massive toll. When you find your financial confidence depleted, it's important to find people to help you make wise decisions. Checking in daily with your finances, reducing spending, and saving regularly are all ways to build confidence in your ability to make, manage, and grow your wealth. Conversely, if you are lucky enough to have more than enough, being generous and giving to others can help boost your financial confidence.

# PROFESSIONAL CONFIDENCE

Professional confidence includes our skill-based abilities. Remarkably, this is one area that can have a huge impact on teams but has a simple remedy. Folks who don't feel equipped to do their job often become unhappy and will seek employment elsewhere. Conversely, you may be seeking employment and unsure of what steps you need to take. Perhaps your company has gone through major changes and you no longer feel as qualified as you once did.

When I left education and stayed home for a few years, I wasn't sure what my return to the workplace would look like. I knew exactly where I wanted to return to — the financial institution where

I'd worked throughout college — but hadn't worked in banking/ finance for a long time. I learned quickly that the best thing you can do when seeking to boost professional confidence is learn to ask for help. Seek out others willing to help guide and mentor you. Be a ravenous consumer of information. Use all the resources available to you from the internet, books, and those who have been working in the industry longer. Don't be afraid to sound stupid. The only dumb question is the one you didn't ask but could have.

---

**The best thing you can do when seeking to boost professional confidence is learn to ask for help.**

---

# HOW OUR CONFIDENCE STORES CAN CHANGE ...

It is my experience that levels of confidence in each area are in a constant state of flux. While I was a stay-at-home mom, my physical, spiritual, and relational confidence (especially as it applied to family) were high. My financial and professional confidence, not so much. During times of transition, our confidence stores can be rapidly depleted and filled ... and can leave us feeling insecure. Moving, starting a new job, losing a job, loss of loved ones, having a child, marriage, and other major transitions in life all cause rapid changes in our confidence and how we balance each area.

Whether we like it or not, each store of confidence can have impact on the others. Being too low in any area can have draining results. When I was growing up, I always heard advice about not bringing your home life to work and vice versa. The harsh reality is that whatever we are dealing with, we carry it with us always. We can exercise emotional control and keep things bottled up, but that can only work for so long. When our confidence stores get depleted, it can bleed over into so many areas.

# MOTOR MOUTH

That was my nickname in elementary school. I'll give you three guesses why. I was the child who, no matter where you sat me, would talk (and talk, and talk). If no other students were seated next to me, it was likely that I would just talk aloud right alongside the teacher. It is safe to say that I was born with a lot of relational confidence. I was always extremely social and never had trouble expressing myself or making friends. I was completely comfortable in a variety of social settings at school, on stage, and wherever I landed. That's why, when my family moved to a new town when I was 11, my parents were shocked when I became quiet and withdrawn. I went from being with my friends every day, chatting nonstop, to having zero friends and being the kid who the teachers were worried about because I didn't talk to anyone. The first several weeks of middle school I went from "motor mouth" to mute. The transition had rapidly depleted my relational confidence.

The tricky thing about confidence is that it's much easier to deplete than replenish. As I pointed out previously, you have to practice what makes you uncomfortable many times before you get comfortable with it. Confidence is the same way. I didn't have enough confidence to put myself out there and be positive, like my mother suggested. Confidence sometimes requires that we test the waters. So I slowly (and sometimes awkwardly) put myself out there at my new school with new peers and started talking. It was awkward at first, but eventually I was back to my old self. I never earned the name "Motor Mouth" at my new school, but it was noted on several report cards that I was "sweet but talkative." During the process, I had to relearn how to introduce myself to other kids, how to build friendships, and navigate social waters. With each new friend, my relational confidence grew.

---

The tricky thing about confidence is that it's much easier to deplete than replenish.

---

# GAINING CONFIDENCE: SOME PRACTICAL TIPS

In the beginning of this book, we talked about our fears. Our confidence stores play a huge part in helping us overcome our fears and get past what holds us back. The good news is that, like our muscles, we can grow each area. How? We grow in confidence by working from our strengths. When we are feeling low in confidence, we likely haven't thought about our strengths for a while. Taking inventory of them will give you a place to work from.

When we think about our strengths, we often think about our accomplishments. But we should also remember to reflect upon the ways we give of ourselves every day; in a world that's all about achievements and tangible results, we tend to overlook our strengths and value when it comes to everyday behaviors. For example, I recently talked to a stay-at-home mom who was looking to reenter the workforce. She said, "I have no confidence. It's been so long since I worked that I've lost all my skill sets." She had all the confidence in the world about being a good mom but couldn't translate that into professional confidence. She asked, "What do I tell them? I'm good at Microsoft Office and great at diaper changes?"

The same may be true for someone who is transitioning from one career to another, from single life to married life, or someone who is adjusting to being a first-time parent. My challenge to my friend was to start listing her strengths — the things she knew she was good at. Then, I asked her to look at them from a different perspective and take her relational strengths and view them from a professional lens. The exercise looked a little like this:

| Strength | Translation |
| --- | --- |
| Making sure household tasks were completed each day | Good at task management |
| Can always fit in workouts between school drop-off, pick-up, sports, meals, bath, and bedtimes | Great at time management and prioritizing |
| Teaches and coordinates Sunday school programs with church | Uses leadership skills to encourage collaboration, and is comfortable teaching and mentoring |

The same "translation exercise" also works in reverse. The strengths that make you stellar professionally often translate in unexpected ways should you choose to apply them to a relational, spiritual, or physical area. It's all about your mindset (there it is again — I told you that mindsets are magical!). Whatever transition you're facing, take inventory of your confidence levels in these five areas: Physical, Spiritual, Relational, Financial, and Professional. Note which areas are feeling depleted and then work from the areas that feel strong. List your strengths and then see how easily they apply to different areas of your life. You will likely surprise yourself. Feeling depleted in all areas? Seek counsel from someone you trust. It is often easier to have others remind us of our strengths than it is to recall them ourselves.

Not only is it important to recognize our own levels of confidence and strength, it's vital that we showcase those strengths to others. When facing organizational changes, viewing them as an opportunity to reveal our strengths to others is important. Let's say the impending change is likely to cause colleagues who are less familiar with technology to struggle. If using technology is a strength of yours, this could be an opportunity for you to show that skill to others and help them through the change. Perhaps an upcoming organizational change means someone will have to take on an extra responsibility. While it may not be ideal, it can be an opportunity to show initiative and demonstrate that you are willing to do more than is expected. Any time you are facing an undesirable change that others dread, use the opportunity to consider how your strengths can make you stand out from the crowd! If you're operating from low confidence in an area relative to the impending change, then keep flexing that muscle and getting out of your comfort zone! Keep tabs on those stores of confidence and do something today to build one of them!

---

**Any time you are facing an undesirable change that others dread, use the opportunity to consider how your strengths can make you stand out from the crowd!**

---

# STRENGTHS

Make a list of your strengths, in any area, and then translate those strengths to areas of your life where you might be less confidence.

## List Strengths

Example: Perhaps one of your professional strengths is a tireless dedication to clients. You know how to get things done when you focus on not wanting to disappoint people you respect.

## Apply Them to a Low-Confidence Area

To gain physical confidence, remind yourself that while 20 minutes on a treadmill might feel foreign, your dedication and discipline in other areas can be translated to physical fitness if you think of yourself (or your body) as a client or "the boss."

**CHAPTER 6**

# Choose Your Attitude, Choose Your Path

*I waited*
*And waited*
*Then waited some more.*
*One day ...*
*Tomorrow ...*
*In the future*
*For sure.*
*Waiting, and waiting, and waiting ...*
*What for?*

In March of 2014, I found myself staring at a contract — in the grips of fear. I was wrapping up my sixth year of teaching. By signing this next contract, I would be committing to my seventh year as an elementary teacher at this public school. My oldest son was about to turn five, my youngest was 10 months old and, despite having signed this ame contract six years in a row, I couldn't escape the giant pit in my stomach. I was more than half-way through the completion of my Master's degree in teacher leadership, and I had no alternative career mapped out. Although I loved children — and teaching — my heart wasn't with the public education system anymore. My head was spinning, thinking about how much time I had invested in my education, the years I'd spent teaching, potentially losing an income if I walked away without a Plan B, and every possible negative scenario. My heart, however, was screaming to take the time with my babies and figure out what would bring me joy. I walked into the principal's office and resigned. I would finish out the current academic year but wouldn't be returning in the fall. I decided to trust God, take a huge risk, and JUMP!

During the next three years, I was busier than ever. I partnered with my husband to launch a small business, West KY ATVs, and together we stretched our entrepreneurial legs. I watched our boys grow. I finished my Master's degree. And reflected as much as I could on where I'd been and where I wanted to go. I had lots of time to determine the type of place I wanted to work for and the kind of people I wanted to work with. The time was challenging financially but, ultimately, it was all worth it. I had spent six years in a job I didn't enjoy, resisting the "change" required of me to chase new dreams and align my life with my aspirations and passions. The experience of avoiding the change and then finally embracing it taught me so much. There are so many reasons we may be resistant to change. There may be relational, financial, or other obstacles that are legitimate challenges. We may never have all the answers and there are times all we can do is take a leap of faith. It may be the best choice you've ever made, or it may be rife with struggles. For me, it was both.

# CURIOUS PATHS, PERFECT DESTINATIONS

As it turns out, being brave enough to change your path is a common denominator among some of the world's most successful people. Famous apparel designer Vera Wang aspired to be a figure skater and later worked as a journalist. She didn't enter the fashion industry until she was 40. Jeff Bezos went from developing computer software for banks to founding Amazon and becoming a billionaire. Iconic actor Harrison Ford was a carpenter for 15 years before deciding to pursue acting. Time and time again, we see examples of the most successful people in the world making major life and career "course corrections" only after those individuals became disenchanted with the paths they were on. So many people, across varying backgrounds and industries, all found success by embracing change and uncertainty. Your greatest happiness and success may be on the other side of a big change too.

Life is funny. Sometimes everything we plan for doesn't quite fit and sometimes amazing things come our way we when we finally allow ourselves to be open. When changes come your way, do you find yourself open or resistant? If you're feeling resistant, do you stop and ask yourself why? Take a mental inventory and explore the reasons the change is bothering you. Maybe it is a fear of failure, or the stress of doing something new. A college professor once told me that every time he felt fear, he asked himself "What is the worst thing that can happen?" He said that the exercise helped him put his fears into perspective. Once he knew the absolute worst thing that could happen, he could then decide if the risk was worth it.

For example, let's pretend the change you are facing is not one you chose. Imagine you are facing a huge change at work that is something unwelcome, like a complete overhaul in process. You've been doing what you do for 20 years and suddenly someone in a suit, in some swanky office, who has no idea how the decision affects everyone, decides to overhaul your process. You are facing an unwelcome change. With any change, you have two pathways that lead to very different results. Let's explore:

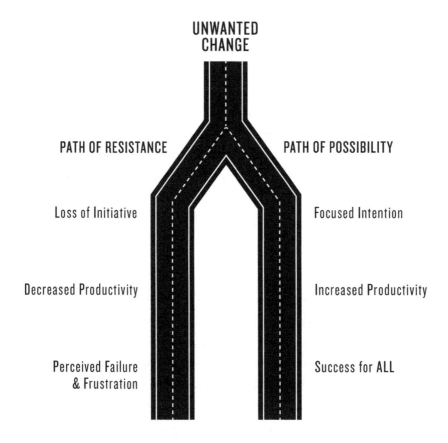

**UNWANTED CHANGE**

PATH OF RESISTANCE

Loss of Initiative

Decreased Productivity

Perceived Failure & Frustration

PATH OF POSSIBILITY

Focused Intention

Increased Productivity

Success for ALL

If the potential outcome of any change carries too great a risk, then it may also be important to stay the course. However, when it comes to small changes at work or home, it is best practice to consider the possibilities right from the start, weigh your options, and decide if the risk is worth it. Often, the risk may come from *not* changing and instead remaining stagnant or on the wrong path. Alternatively, the risk may be too great but change still inevitable. In this case, you can now look at other options and perhaps consider some things you hadn't allowed yourself to consider before.

Before I say more about the two paths — the Path of Resistance and the Path of Possibility — it's important that we take a time-out for me to clarify something critical. You've heard me cheerlead for change, again and again, in this book. But not all changes are positive and not all people attempting to persuade you to change have your interests at heart. There will be times — in work and in life — to hold fast to your instincts and *resist* change, sometimes vehemently, with all your might. I'm talking about when changes present challenges to your personal integrity, beliefs, or values ... or worse, when a "change" violates your safety or dignity, when it violates the law, or when it presents you or others with danger. Never let your aspirations to be a Change Embracer violate your sense of self or your self-worth.

# THE PATH OF RESISTANCE

The Path of Resistance is our default setting when facing an unwelcome change. We are hardwired to resist. When we are comfortable and then someone introduces an unwelcome change to our daily routine, our fight-or-flight response kicks in. In work or with family, "flight" isn't always an option so we choose to fight and begin the long road down the Path of Resistance. Let's explore common stops along the Path of Resistance.

## Loss of Initiative

This first stop is also our first indicator that we are on the Path of Resistance. When faced with an unwelcome change, we are apt to feel a mix of emotions like frustration, anger, and even resentment because we can't run. Our world has been turned upside down at work or at home and instead of battling it out, we feel like giving up. Because life didn't bother to ask us how we feel about this change, we simply don't care anymore. Loss of initiative sets in and we simply stop striving toward our best. This may present itself as doing the bare minimum to get by. When we're here, we feel like what we're doing just doesn't matter. At this point, we're simply going through the motions.

Loss of initiative can happen on the Path of Resistance whether the change we're facing is personal or professional. As a personal example, imagine your doctor puts you on a medication that has a side effect of weight gain and fatigue. It's suddenly harder to stay fit and trim, and you feel like giving up. You have no initiative regarding exercise or diet because it's too hard now. Why try? Eat another cookie, Cancel the health club membership.

Loss of initiative happens when we resist change at work too. I once had a colleague who, despite being very skilled, had simply checked out. She was a talented and dependable worker but, over time, staffing changes had led to some discouragement on her part. She sought advancement but had not been granted the promotions she desired. Instead of continuing to excel where she was, she backtracked. She showed up to work, but had checked out emotionally and intellectually. She had lost all initiative to do any more than the bare minimum. Unfortunately, the resulting loss of initiative was like a neon sign saying, "Don't promote me." Instead of asking what she could do better and attempting to grow and be her best, she had simply shut down.

## Decreased Productivity

When we lack initiative over time, we end up with decreased productivity. Because we no longer care about *what* we're doing, we're no longer in a hurry to achieve and, as a result, everything starts to slow down. Have you heard the phrase "One bad apple can spoil the bunch?" Well, that's what starts to happen when we reach a point of decreased productivity — our slow-down and our failure to "give a darn" starts to have measurable, negative impact on the people and organizations around us. When we're thinking clearly and not working hard to resist change, most of us would admit that we have a shared desire to have healthy relationships at work and at home. But when we feel unproductive in one area, it can slowly seep into another and, suddenly, relationships are in jeopardy. Being unproductive also affects the confidence stores we talked about in Chapter 5 and can slowly deplete each one. We may feel (at least subconsciously) like being less productive is a smart strategy to make others see that the change was a bad idea, but we are rarely accomplishing anything other than sabotaging ourselves.

Let's revisit my colleague mentioned above — the woman who checked out after she got passed over for a promotion. Decreased productivity was inevitable for her as she traveled the Path of Resistance because she had lost *all* initiative. She quickly earned a reputation for taking all available sick and vacation time as soon as it was accrued and doing the bare minimum to get by. And it wasn't just her coworkers who saw the impact of her resistance ... the customers suffered too. My colleague's customer service quality began to diminish and, because she was a seasoned team member to whom others once looked for guidance and cultural cues, her behaviors began setting an unhealthy example for new employees. At her core, she wanted to feel successful but her resistance to the changes happening around her at work only compounded her problems.

## Perceived Failure and Frustration

The final stop on the Path of Resistance leaves us dead in the water. When human initiative is lost and productivity decreases, the entire project or change can fall apart. We may find ourselves in a truly discouraging place — realizing that the change (which might have been full of opportunity or at least necessary) was unsuccessful because we never gave it a chance to succeed in the first place. Those who wanted the change to succeed are unhappy and those of us who resisted the change are also unhappy ... because we aren't being our best selves. It is in this cesspool of frustration that relationships and entire teams are irreparably damaged. When we've reached this stage, the process has become fractured to the point of disaster. The point we thought we were making — the message we were trying to send to others by being resistant — was lost and everyone has suffered.

One of the most disheartening things I noticed about my former colleague was how her frustration permeated throughout the workplace culture and impacted those around her. She became a magnet for gossip — welcoming it and perpetuating it. And in most encounters she had with others, she was just oozing with obvious frustration. She perceived the staffing changes around her (and also the *lack* of changes she wanted to see) as a failure instead of an opportunity. This failure mindset affected everyone around her.

Does this sound familiar? I'd wager that we've all experienced this proverbial dead end at some point in our professional or personal lives — where we're stuck, not because the change was doomed to fail or wasn't a good idea, but because the *people* along the path of change chose resistance instead of possibility. When you think about the unwelcome, unexpected changes or disappointments that affect our day-to-day comfort, I want you to think *not* about the path of resistance but of a *better* path. There is a path that allows you to speak your mind and to do so with credibility. Let me introduce you to the Path of Possibility.

# THE PATH OF POSSIBILITY

## Focused Intention

When you choose to walk the Path of Possibility, amazing things happen. Instead of losing your sense of initiative, you will approach the change with focused intention. Focused intention *is not* relinquishing yourself to the inevitable. Instead, it is taking the time to fully understand the goal behind the change and the challenges ahead. Unwelcome changes, whether they are organizational or personal, often create high emotions because of the element of surprise. When we use focused intention, we channel that emotion into action and create a plan for moving forward. Ask yourself: "What is your true intention moving forward?" If your emotions are telling you that the change will be overwhelming, take time to map out the extra workload over time. Think about how you can leverage change as an opportunity for growth. Write down your intention and next steps.

---

**Focused intention is *not* relinquishing yourself to the inevitable. Instead, it is taking the time to fully understand the goal behind the change and the challenges ahead.**

---

I again want to use my former colleague as an example here. Had she faced the change with focused intention, sought feedback, and worked to grow instead of shutting down, her results would have been different. She would have taken the disappointment and let it fuel her goals. She could have been a source of inspiration for others, rather than a distractor and a source of workplace toxicity.

# Increased Productivity

Increased productivity is a byproduct of using high emotions to focus
our intentions instead of becoming stagnant. When we have focused
our intention into developing next steps, we can begin working
*through* the change instead of against it. Using our intentions to guide
our actions results in higher levels of motivation. We start generating
results (i.e., the intention becomes productivity) and that feeling of
accomplishment fuels additional personal productivity and ripples
throughout the team or organization, creating productivity for others.
Working through change with increased productivity allows everyone
to approach challenges with a solutions-based mindset. Instead
of focusing on problems, we begin to create solutions that benefit
all involved.

---

**Working through change with increased
productivity allows everyone to approach
challenges with a solutions-based mindset.**

---

Had my former colleague exercised focused intention from the start,
she would have found a huge increase in her productivity. Instead
of shutting down and giving up, she would have gotten to work and
made herself invaluable to those around her. This kind of increase in
productivity would have made it impossible to pass her up for future
opportunities!

# Success for All

What does success look like in your situation? What desired outcome
did you identify while focusing your intentions? Perhaps the end
goal is to "meet numbers" (e.g., sales volume, profit margin, work

productivity or however your organization measures your work) without increasing your workload. Maybe you want to finally land that promotion. Your unwelcome change may have left you wanting to repair relationships, either personal or professional. Regardless of your chosen goals, staying focused on the Path of Possibility means greater chance of success for all. Your accomplishments not only set an example for others, but they also make the overall transition easier. While the Path of Resistance only leads to perceived failure and frustration, the Path of Possibility creates a greater chance of success for everyone.

In an ideal world, my colleague would have followed the Path of Possibility and others would have watched her grow, thrive, and succeed. Not only would she have accomplished her goals, but she would have inspired others to do the same. She would have taken to change and disappointment and allowed it to make her better. Instead of blaming her supervisors, she would have taken ownership over the situation and grown from it. Blame, bitterness, and resentment don't serve you. Let go of those things and set yourself on the Path of Possibility.

---

**Blame, bitterness, and resentment don't serve you.**

---

## THE CHOICE IS YOURS

Making drastic changes in our lives is scary but without change, there can't be growth. Maybe you're comfortable doing things as you've always done them. Perhaps you don't see any reason to change. I understand — the status quo is sometimes easy ... it requires no thought or commitment. But consider this, if you ever feel worry or anxiety, stop and ask yourself if making a change could help. I'd like to put the Path of Resistance and the Path of Possibility in another context for you. Let's use Bob as a hypothetical example. Bob is in his 40s and struggles with anxiety. He doesn't love his job because he thinks he is being overlooked by management and not moving forward at the pace he hoped for his career. Now, Bob is being told he must learn to operate a new software system while maintaining his current production levels. He knows that learning the new system will create added stress that will likely affect his numbers in the short term, but Bob has never been outspoken. He is fearful that sharing his feelings with his boss would cause conflict or disappointment. He is so stressed that he has gained 20 pounds and has been looking for new jobs but can't find one within his field near his home. If Bob follows the Path of Resistance, he will continue to feel stagnant, be stressed, and possibly gain more weight or develop other health problems. Bob may ultimately be terminated from his job because his supervisor will see his resistance and negative behaviors as a lack of motivation and commitment.

---

**Making drastic changes in our lives is scary but without change, there can't be growth.**

---

But what if Bob chooses a different path? If Bob follows the Path of Possibility, he will focus his intentions and speak up to his supervisor about how he's feeling. He'll approach the conversation with a map for learning the new software system on a timetable that makes sense for him. His supervisor might immediately take interest in the change in Bob's behavior and assure Bob that his work is appreciated and if he keeps this positive, can-do attitude, he'll be a shoo-in for the next promotion. With the weight of worry off Bob's shoulders, he stops "stress eating" and his weight normalizes. He feels hopeful and at peace about the future — all because of one tiny choice (though truly huge in impact!) to approach the workplace change from a different perspective and traveling a positive path of possibility.

When we make the conscious choice to go down the Path of Possibility, we are looking at the unwelcome change through a new lens. We are choosing to explore the possibilities associated with the change instead of focusing only on perceived difficulty. We are doing so by using focused intention. With focused intention, we may still have negative thoughts or feelings, but we actively focus our intention on the best possible outcome and drive toward that. Focused intention gives us the opportunity to turn fear into conviction that drives change.

---

**When we make the conscious choice to go down the Path of Possibility, we are looking at the unwelcome change through a new lens. We are choosing to explore the possibilities associated with the change instead of focusing only on perceived difficulty.**

---

Make no mistake. What seems like a tiny change or small jump to one person might seem like a huge death-defying feat to another. Choosing a different path doesn't mean there won't be difficulty and high emotions. It does mean that we use those emotions to move ourselves forward in a healthy way. If what you are currently doing isn't working for you or you aren't happy, then you are likely on the Path of Resistance. Fortunately, it's never too late to make another choice. Getting started is always the hardest part of any change. We are programmed to reject what makes us uncomfortable. Choosing the Path of Possibility over the Path of Resistance takes practice and the willingness to consistently examine our choices as we navigate change. And there's no time like now to start practicing.

---

It's never too late to make another choice.

---

# THE TIME IS NOW

There are always changes happening all around you ... ones that have been put in motion by other people and to which you need to respond. And there are changes on your mind and on the horizon. They all need your attention.

When should you speak up?

When should you start?

When is the right time to make a different choice?

The answer is *the moment you realize the path you're currently on isn't working or won't work for much longer.* Change takes time, so the sooner you get the wheels turning, the better. There will always be reasons to *not* start making different choices. You may be extremely busy; things may be hectic at work; someone else may be urging you to wait to satisfy their own agenda. Regardless of the situation, it will rarely be made better by putting it off. If you are working through a welcome change, or you're preparing for a change you didn't ask for, the time to start is *now*.

Because I work in talent development — helping people improve their knowledge, attitudes, skills, and habits — I often get asked questions by people seeking career advancement. I recently had a conversation with a woman who had aspired to a specific position. She knew the requirements, qualifications, and what she was lacking in terms of her work experience. We even had a program designed to train someone in the exact skills needed for the position she sought.

Her question was simply "When do you think I should start?" My answer was obviously "NOW!" No, there wasn't an immediate job opening for her or guarantees that if she completed the training program, she would land the position, but there were free resources right at her fingertips! And those resources were designed to help her grow in the direction she was leaning. She had all the tools but simply needed the extra nudge (or even permission) to go ahead and get started.

Think of any change like a mountain. Now whether you have chosen to climb this mountain for fun or for sport, or if it has been placed in front of you, is irrelevant because you simply want to get over the mountain successfully. Presumably, you'd like to get to the other side of the mountain easily, safely, and without incident. You would take the time to learn what you need to get over the mountain, prepare for the weather, study, gather tools and equipment. But once you have what you need, you wouldn't stand and stare at the mountain expecting it to move. Start climbing!

# CHOOSING YOUR PATH

**What change are you avoiding that would make your personal or work life better?**

_____

_____

_____

_____

_____

**What is the first step you can take to start on a better path?**

_____

_____

_____

_____

_____

## CHAPTER 7

# Kick It into Overdrive

*I've got this thing*
*I need to do.*
*You may even have one too.*
*I dread it so ...*
*It's awfully hard*
*To find the perfect place to start.*
*I could start here,*
*Or maybe there.*
*I really can't decide on where.*
*Now that one thing*
*Has turned to two ...*
*Now I don't know what to do.*
*Two to three,*
*Now three to four.*
*Maybe I should have started before.*

When I was five, I attended a daycare facility called Kinder College. I don't remember much about the daycare center, other than the fact that they had a pool and it terrified me. During the summer, all the kids and teachers would go to the pool for hours and I would sit on the side ... with just my feet in the water. If someone dared to come near me, I would pull my feet out and scoot over so that I wasn't in contact with the water or at risk of being pulled in. Everyone tried to coax me in — my mother, all the other teachers, and even some of the older kids. They constantly tried to get me to come in, using floats or water wings to keep me safe and confident. But I would not move. It didn't matter how many flotation devices or goggles I had. I dreaded getting anywhere near the water. It was a crippling fear.

I can remember the feeling of missing out (known today as FOMO — "fear of missing out"), wanting so badly to experience the fun all the other kids were having, but being too afraid to do so. I can't remember what exactly changed in me but one day, with no one looking, no one urging me, everyone gathered at the other end of the pool, I slid in with my water wings and floated like a human buoy. I didn't move, the fear was still there, but doggone it I was in the water! Bobbing in place. It wasn't nearly as bad as I had imagined. In fact, it was *fun*! All that dread and nervousness was for nothing.

Procrastination works the same way. The dread we build up while avoiding doing whatever it is we don't want to do becomes much worse than the action or change itself. In grade school, I would have weeks to complete a project and wait until the night before. I would spend the weeks leading up to the project worrying, stressing and fretting over it instead of getting it done and enjoying the time I had. The cruel irony of procrastination is that it doesn't delay or diminish our problems ... it multiplies them. When we avoid issues demanding our attention, they get bigger or more urgent. Then we are avoiding *more* things until we are so stressed that we panic.

The cruel irony of procrastination is that it doesn't delay
or diminish our problems ... it multiplies them.

# THE "DOING" METHOD OF TAMING PROCRASTINATION

Perhaps you have convinced yourself that you "work best under pressure." As I've mentioned, I have a true distaste for that phrase. While it may be true from time to time (and in very specific circumstances) that people can perform and thrive under pressures they could have avoided by not procrastinating, most of life's responsibilities will pile up quickly and cause unnecessary stress if left until the last minute. The reality of procrastination and "working under pressure" is that it creates higher levels of stress that our bodies and minds must cope with. At work, we may procrastinate on reports, emails, quarterly or yearly tasks, scheduling meetings that might be difficult, etc. At home, it may be laundry, dishes, repairing the fence, working on a family budget, helping our kids practice for the spelling bee, and so forth. My personal kryptonite is laundry. I am convinced that nudist colonies are a direct result of not wanting to do laundry. For years, we struggled with what we affectionately dubbed "Mount Laundry" — the giant pile that lived in our laundry room. I would buy hampers, dividers, pin things on Pinterest, and yet Mt. Laundry endured. It took me *way* too long to realize that the issue wasn't in the organization (i.e., it couldn't be resolved with the perfect hamper). The issue was in the *doing*. Anyone who knows me knows that I have made a complete turnaround when it comes to procrastination. I can't *stand* to procrastinate. In fact, now I am usually way ahead of schedule on everything. So, what's the difference? What is the secret sauce ... the magic pill ... the ultimate fix for procrastination everywhere? It is a little acronym I lovingly refer to as DOING. All the magic lies in the **DOING**. Let me explain ...

**D – Dump**. Dump all your thoughts, worries, goals, and to-dos on paper. It doesn't have to be pretty, or make sense, just get it out.

**O – Order**. Order each thought and to-do by urgency. Categories could be DO NOW, DO IN A FEW DAYS, DO LATER, or whatever works for you. Highest-priority items need to be first on the list.

**I – Invest**. Invest your time. Whether you have a little or a lot, resolve to take advantage of each block of time you have available.

**N – Neutralize**. Neutralize distractions. Set yourself up for success by putting your smartphone on Do Not Disturb, playing some music to help you focus, and finding a place where others won't be tempted to distract you.

**G – Go!** Just get started. Starting is the hardest part. Rip off the bandage, as they say, and get going! When we are facing a change or trying to make a change, the difference between success and failure lies in the "doing." We can dream big, buy all the planners, talk it out, and research something to death without ever making any headway. If we wait for all the stars to align and for things to be perfect, then we miss out on opportunities to forge ahead. Perfection is the enemy of progress. Changing, growing, and getting better can only happen when we're brave enough to step out into the uncomfortable unknown.

# DUMP: HOW TO GET WORRIES AND THOUGHTS OUT OF YOUR HEAD

Let's explore each phase of DOING a little further. **DUMP** is the first phase in DOING. You're going to dump all those thoughts, ideas, and to-do's out on paper (or computer). This helps eliminate distractions and give everything a focus. If you're facing a change at work that you haven't asked for, writing all the steps down on paper can help alleviate the anxiety of what's to come. Often, when we're facing change or trying to make lasting changes, the worry of it all can be stressful and even interfere with our sleep. I find it particularly beneficial to keep something on my nightstand to purge any thoughts of to-do's right before bed. Dumping your thoughts in a digital device or on paper gives your mind the chance to rest. Suddenly, all those thoughts that were swimming around creating chaos are now safely stored. By dumping the thoughts, you are giving your brain permission to let them go until you need them.

One of my personal favorite ways to dump thoughts is the notes app on my phone. If something pops in my head at the grocery store, while sleeping, anytime or anywhere, I can safely record it in my phone and whatever worry it presented will pass. My brain feels tremendous pressure to remember all the details from my day. From work, projects, schedules for the office, schedules for my family, doctors' appointments, and countless other things, it is easy to feel mental overload trying to keep up with it all. It seems so silly but there is magic in housing every to-do, thought, or worry somewhere physical (a notebook, a computer, a smartphone, a scrap of paper) so your brain can take a breather! Once the worry has gone from my mind and has been relocated into digital notes, I won't worry about it anymore. I'm free to continue sleeping, spending time with my kiddos, or focusing on the present.

# ORDER: GETTING DELIBERATE ABOUT WHAT MATTERS AND WHAT TAKES PRIORITY

After dumping all those thoughts, ideas, and to-do's, the next step is **ORDER**. Once you have all those pesky thoughts out, you can begin to think about them in order of importance. Ordering is the step that will help you act on what matters the most. When you take the time to order your thoughts, you are ensuring that what you choose to focus on aligns with your goals. How you choose to order those thoughts looks different for everyone. You can order those thoughts by most important to least important, assign deadlines to each, place them into categories; whatever works for you, *do it*! Ordering all those thoughts and to-do's will help your brain begin to focus on what is within your immediate control and what isn't. Not only does it create focus, but it also allows you to release thoughts that don't serve you. You've recognized them, realized you can't control them, and now you can move on from them.

Personally, I like to order all those notes and thoughts into three categories: do now, do later, and backburner. Anything that doesn't require an action or response on my part is deemed not worthy of my attention and is scratched off the list. In some ways, when I go through the process of bringing order to my thoughts, I am agreeing to myself to only focus on what really matters to me and what I can control. When I have a thought or worry that is outside of my control and put it on paper, it very clearly shows to me that it is unimportant in terms of my attention; it's out of my control so therefore off my list. I'm able to process the fleeting thought and let it go. It's a great way to acknowledge those thoughts that don't serve you and focus your time and energy on what is important.

# INVEST: CARVING OUT TIME FOR PROGRESS AND POSSIBILITY

The third step is **INVEST**. It's time to get started! I wasn't kidding when I said, "Starting is the hardest part." That's because any great change is going to demand an investment of your time. Coincidentally, time is the one thing most of us seem to feel like we don't have enough of. This is especially true during change. It takes motivation to start carving out time for what you want, and the best motivation is to remember your "why." Why are you tackling this? What are your goals? What do you hope to achieve? Think of change again as a mountain. To get over it, you must get going!

---

**Any great change is going to demand an investment of your time. Coincidentally, time is the one thing most of us seem to feel like we don't have enough of.**

---

Let's say you're facing a process change at work and it is completely overwhelming. List out everything standing in your way and get started attacking the items one at a time. Maybe you have a goal in mind, but it is going to take a lot of hard work and determination to get there. The best part about the INVEST phase is that you've got nowhere to go but up! With each small victory, you'll gain more confidence and what seemed like a mountain before doesn't seem so large or daunting after all. Pretty soon, you'll feel more in control of your time and will, in turn, have more time to spare.

The best way to figure out how to carve out more time is to look at how you're currently spending your time. Break each day down into 10-minute segments (yes, I said 10 minutes). Look at how you're spending each of those 10 minutes. Could you wake up 30 minutes earlier to work on a project you've been meaning or needing to do? Could you take 10 minutes away from social media to fit in a workout? Could time on the commuter train be spent listening to audio books? Could time in waiting rooms be spent catching up with a friend or family member via text? To find time, you must really examine how you're currently spending it and be completely honest with yourself. Remember, you have the same amount of time in the day as every successful person in the world. It's all about how you invest it. Remember Mt. Laundry? I didn't even have to create extra time to deal with it! There were already pockets of time when my husband, kids, and I would gather in the living room and watch a movie or show together. This was the *perfect* time to tackle the folding of the laundry together without getting up early or staying up late. Look for times when you can add in something productive without adding hours to the day.

---

**Remember, you have the same amount of time in the day as every successful person in the world. It's all about how you invest it.**

---

Remember, we find time to invest when something is truly important to us. That doesn't mean important to someone else. We are inundated daily with messages that tell us what we should do, how we should look, what should be on our minds or in our hearts — we hear those messages on television and social media, from our friend, from retailers bombarding our mailboxes and our email inboxes. But regardless of what others are telling you, you must be keenly aware of what really matters to *you*. Reevaluate your values, your goals, and what important targets you have in mind to understand how to invest your time. When an organization is facing a significant change, communicating how team members should invest their time is crucial. If you are unsure how to spend your day or your week in the wake of (or in anticipation of) a big change at work or at home, take time to dump your thoughts, order them based on what you know, and invest your time accordingly.

---

If you are unsure how to spend your day or your week in the wake of (or in anticipation of) a big change at work or at home, take time to dump your thoughts, order them based on what you know, and invest your time accordingly.

---

## NEUTRALIZE: SLAYING YOUR DISTRACTIONS SO YOU CAN FOCUS

By now you've dumped your thoughts, ordered your priorities, and invested your time. You're well on your way to knocking this change out of the park! The fourth part of DOING is **NEUTRALIZE**. To make the most of the time you will be investing, you must neutralize distractions. I love that my phone now tells me how much screen time I have each day and week. I mentioned in Chapter 2 that this feature allows me to reduce my social media exposure and help kick "social comparisons" (those pressures to keep up with the proverbial Joneses). The screen-time data on my phone also helps me accomplish my overall DOING because it lets me know, without question, that I need to limit overall screen-time distractions to get more accomplished. There are some distractions that are unavoidable, so focus on what you can control. I have a set number of hours each day where my phone is on "do not disturb." Friends and family can call or text, but it won't come through. As a result, I get a set amount of uninterrupted time with my kiddos *and* uninterrupted sleep time as well.

---

## To make the most of the time you will be investing, you must neutralize distractions.

---

When I was in my twenties, I had my second child, was working full time, and took a full course-load of graduate-level courses. I thought I was going to go insane! I had all kinds of distractions and was completely boggled as to how I could neutralize all of them. I realized it would be impossible to carve out time every day for my schoolwork and that one day a week was all I had. So, instead of neutralizing distractions every day, I took each Saturday for the entire year and walled myself off in a room from 6:00 a.m. until 6:00 p.m., studying and working on projects for my Master's program. I would cram in an entire week's worth of schoolwork on Saturday and, if it was a light week, I would begin on the next week's work. This wasn't easy, especially without enough sleep (and I always seemed to be sleep-deprived), but I knew that it was necessary to complete the program.

Often, when we are having difficulty making a change, we like to use unavoidable distractions as an excuse. There may be reports due that we feel are unnecessary, family members who call too frequently, an injury that gets in the way of physical goals, babies keeping us up at night, and so on. These distractions are real and often unavoidable. Instead of focusing on how those distractions keep us from our goals, we would be wise to focus on what is within our control and recognize when we are intentionally choosing a distraction to avoid the inevitable. Focus on solutions instead of problems.

# GO: TAKE THE FIRST STEP, AND THEN KEEP GOING

The fifth and final phase of the DOING method for taming procrastination is **GO**! Nike had it right when they said, "Just do it!" At the end of the day, when you know your priorities, have mapped out your steps, and are ready, you simply must get started and keep going! American fast-food tycoon Ray Kroc is said to have repeatedly asked, "Are you green and growing or ripe and rotten?" This is one of my favorite quotes. Change is constant. Once you've successfully navigated one change and conquered one goal, it's time to move on to the next one!

When I was young, I had a horrible fear of removing Band-Aids. Being a clumsy child, however, I used more Band-Aids than I would have liked. It never failed that I would leave the Band-Aid on for days and days past when it was necessary because I was afraid it would hurt if we took it off. As an adult, I can't seem to get a Band-Aid to stay in place, but, as a child, they were felt permanently glued to my skin. I remember my mother negotiating with me to remove the Band-Aids. I never wanted her to remove them quickly and would instead spend lots of time slowly peeling them off my skin. This, no doubt, inflicted much more pain than was necessary. Inevitably, I learned that even though it still sometimes hurt to remove a Band-Aid quickly, I was deciding to make the discomfort last longer, and that was just illogical. So I learned to grimace and pull!

Change is the same way. The GO step of the DOING method illustrates the importance of ripping off the Band-Aid and getting started, even when we're inclined to procrastinate. Change is uncomfortable. We must deploy techniques that make the process more bearable. The DOING method is how I personally start each week — and sometimes each day, depending on what immediate goals I have or the changes I'm trying to make. Not surprisingly, the more I implement the DOING process, the more I accomplish! Whenever life gets chaotic or I feel overwhelmed, it is also the process that re-centers everything and gets me back to a place of peace. Changes come with lots of steps and to-dos. I promise that if you use the DOING process to get a handle on them, great things will happen!

---

### Change is uncomfortable. We must deploy techniques that make the process more bearable.

---

# DUMP & ORDER

**Dump all your thoughts below.**

_____

_____

_____

_____

_____

**Now, sort them into the categories below.**

| Important to Do Now | Do Later | Unimportant |
| --- | --- | --- |
| | | |

## CHAPTER 8

# Managing the Road Ahead

*Up, Work, Sleep, Repeat ...*
*Every day is such a feat.*
*The wheel turns left,*
*The wheel turns right,*
*Work all day,*
*Sleep at night.*
*Running here,*
*Running there ...*
*Somehow ending up nowhere.*

One of the things that makes change so difficult is how uncomfortable it is to break habits and build new ones. Every day is a new opportunity to face change head-on and conquer it. So why don't we? Winston Churchill said, "Plans are of little importance, but planning is essential." When we don't spend time planning, our brains switch to autopilot. We simply go through the motions and hope for decent results.

---

**One of the things that makes change so difficult is how uncomfortable it is to break habits and build new ones.**

---

Allowing your brain to go on autopilot can have interesting consequences. After my second son was born, I was dangerously sleep deprived. New parents will agree that life still goes on whether you have slept or not. Work still needed to be done, our oldest needed to get to school, and the mission each day was to survive. When you've had very little sleep, you really cling to the routines you've established previously. Good or bad, my one morning routine has always been to have a cup of coffee. This certainly didn't change with sleep deprivation. In fact, it increased exponentially.

One weekday morning, after not enough sleep, I stumbled into the kitchen in my pajamas and slippers with a baby on my hip. It was 6:00 a.m. and time to get our oldest (and myself) ready to go. I needed coffee! Every coffee routine was the same. Grab mug, place mug on stand, grab coffee pod, insert coffee pod, grab creamer from refrigerator while coffee was brewing, add creamer, drink coffee, rise from the dead. Same routine every morning. As a result, my brain was completely on autopilot when going through the routine. However, this particular morning, there was a certain element of that routine out of place. Instead of the coffee creamer being where it always was, it had been replaced. "What was in its place?" you ask? Chicken stock. You know, the salty chicken broth that comes in a cardboard box with a tiny spout. Yep ... that stuff. I poured it into my coffee. I even stirred it in. It never occurred to me that the coffee didn't lighten in color or I didn't smell that hint of vanilla. My brain was on autopilot and the results were, well, less than appetizing.

When it comes to facing change, autopilot is the enemy. Autopilot makes us become stagnant and more prone to mistakes. In organizations, autopilot can cost a ton of money! I once watched a YouTube video where a factory worker who had been used to stamping parts that came through the line was moved to a section of the line where parts were inspected for mistakes. His brain was still on autopilot and many mistakes went unnoticed because his brain was still in stamping mode. He was even observed on footage raising his hand to stamp and pressing parts he should have been sorting. It was his routine. What does your routine look like? Is it helping you navigate change or holding you back? If you aren't sure, here are a few tips to help you.

---

## When it comes to facing change, autopilot is the enemy.

---

# BREAK IT APART

Every change seems like a long and arduous journey at first. Whether unexpected and unwelcome or a goal we'd like to achieve and want to embrace, change can seem completely overwhelming. There is an old saying: "How do you eat an elephant? One bite at a time." Change requires time, and small bites. Thankfully, time gives us the opportunity to take that which seems overwhelming and break it apart into manageable pieces. Overhauling your entire routine at once isn't sustainable. Instead, identify what is manageable for you and start there. Break apart the tasks, the challenge, the change at hand into manageable pieces.

For example, if you're facing a process change at work, identify what you will need to learn and practice to become proficient. Take what you've identified and turn it into a monthly, weekly, and even a daily plan to get from point A to point B without becoming overwhelmed. The same applies to personal changes and goals as well. If you've never tried distance running, chances are you won't be marathon ready in a day. You must start with small achievable goals. That's what makes programs like Couch to 5K so effective. They break those huge tasks down into small, bite-sized pieces. This keeps overwhelm to a minimum. The best part is that you can do the same thing with any change you're facing (e.g., weight loss, starting a blog, learning a new job, earning a degree, training a new employee, overseeing a home-renovation project).

What change are you facing that needs your attention right now? Is it a welcome change or one you dread? Think about the big picture and the timeframe you're working with. If the change must take place over a few days, break those days into hours where you can work on learning and developing a little at a time. If you have weeks or months to make the change, assign weekly goals and plan each day to hit the smaller targets over time. Learning to see the big picture and then breaking it into manageable pieces is a skill that helps you avoid overwhelm and burnout.

## START WITH THE MORNING

Oh, the morning. It seems like there are two types of people in this world — those who are morning people and those who are not. I am the latter. Whether you innately love mornings or not, it still stands that the way you start each day sets the tone for the rest of it. Mornings also tend to be some of the only flexible hours we have at our disposal as we try to build better habits. How do you spend your mornings? Are you in a fog, letting your brain take you through the motions on autopilot? Are your mornings rushed and chaotic, trying to scramble out the door on time? So many people have tackled the topic of making the most of your mornings. There are countless books, blogs, vlogs, webinars, and social media wisdom dedicated to making you successful by helping you master a morning routine.

Your morning doesn't have to look like anyone else's. Remember, the reason we are looking to find time in the morning is to work toward whatever goal we have in mind. It isn't about copying someone else's morning routine. Instead, it is about crafting a morning routine that works for *you*, helps you navigate changes easier, and sets you up for positivity throughout the day. Your morning will look different depending on your situation and what you value. In addition, morning routines *change*! My morning routine changes drastically when my sons are in school or if I'm traveling. Regardless, I typically read every morning over a cup of coffee. I also try to schedule most of my work calls in the morning so I can complete "focused work" during the midday.

Every morning is a fresh opportunity to give yourself extra time, set your mind right, and get one step closer to your destination. This may involve getting up earlier or it may not. If your mornings are super rushed, you could probably use the extra time. Some people love mornings for a quick workout and quiet time to start the day off with a clear head. Decide what exactly makes your morning worthwhile and be intentional about it each day.

> Every morning is a fresh opportunity to give yourself extra time, set your mind right, and get one step closer to your destination.

In my career in elementary education and now corporate training, one of the unique things I have had the opportunity to observe is how teams build morning routines and the impact it has on their ability to navigate change together. I've noticed a direct correlation between morning routines of teams and the overall culture. Teams that begin the day discussing do's, don'ts, task-based information, and so forth tend to have *more* difficulty connecting their work to purpose, despite it seeming like a morning meeting of any kind could be beneficial. Likewise, teams that don't have a morning routine but simply start working away tend to feel disconnected and under-valued. However, teams that take the time to connect, share praises, read, and give coworkers time to weigh-in on decisions face change and its challenges with much more success. It stands to reason that a positive morning routine, whether personal or professional, sets the tone for the rest of the day.

# PLAN YOUR DAY

Have you ever heard the expression "building the plane while flying it?" It's one of those phrases that always made me cringe. One, because I don't like flying and, two, people often say this to hide the fact that they really don't know what they're doing. It doesn't sound like a way I'd like to fly or do much of anything for that matter. Yet, that is exactly how most people and teams start every single day. No plan, no direction, no "fully built plane" — just tackling things as they come up, "flying" and hoping the wings don't fall off. Sound familiar? I've heard so many people say, "I've been working all day and haven't gotten anything accomplished." If most of your day feels like you're putting out fires and not achieving what you'd like, then you need to start with a daily plan. This is especially important in times of change because the daily plan is what keeps your "why" at the forefront of all that you do. It also makes it easier to say "yes" or "no" to things depending on whether they align with your plan.

The actual process of starting your day by planning is like turning off your brain's faulty autopilot. The planning process refocuses us and allows us to prioritize our goals into the framework of the day. Daily plans can be simple or elaborate, paper or digital; you should do whatever works best for you. Remember, you aren't doing this planning just to have things written in a planner or saved somewhere digitally. You're planning because the *process* of it is where you reap the rewards. My personal daily plan involves both paper-based and digital steps. Studies show that the act of putting pen to paper helps commit information to memory. That's why, although I have each day's appointments on my digital calendar, I also take time to write out on paper what I'm grateful for, goals, top three priorities for the day, and my schedule. This helps set me up for success.

---

## Starting your day by planning is like turning off your brain's faulty autopilot.

---

When planning your day, consider separating what must be done right away versus what can wait until later. Look at each hour you have available and see where you can find time to work toward your goals, brush up on work skills, practice, or learn something new. Take advantage of your time and commit to your plan by not allowing others' emergencies to get in your way. It may seem difficult at first but planning each day, when practiced over time, means less time putting out fires and more time heading in a positive direction. You inevitably will be much more focused on each task, knowing that you planned it because it has purpose and because it will help you achieve your goals. This kind of planning also reduces your stress and leads to increased productivity at home and at work.

When you spend time planning, each task you commit to is proactive instead of reactive; each task, therefore, has purpose and is more likely to get accomplished. You feel prepared to say "no" or "not right now" when you can explain to others what you're working toward and when you'll be able to make time for them as well. It prevents dialogue that haphazardly commits you to things that aren't getting you where you want to go. Daily planning may seem extreme, but it is one of those magical, life-changing habits that makes all the difference in navigating change and being successful. Feeling skeptical? Give it a try for one week and see what happens.

---

**When you spend time planning, each task you commit to is proactive instead of reactive; each task, therefore, has purpose and is more likely to get accomplished.**

---

Daily planning isn't just an "individual sport" — it's vital for teams too! Daily planning in a team setting is an extremely powerful tool when it comes to helping your organization navigate changes. It gives everyone an opportunity to voice concerns, solve problems together, and own a piece of the puzzle. Big team achievements are made possible by setting daily goals together. A colleague and manager that I am blessed to work with has mastered planning in a team setting. She is stellar at using meeting times to plan with and involve her entire team. She uses existing meeting times and takes advantage of having everyone together to accomplish more. Everyone knows the plan, has an opportunity for input, knows their role, and knows the desired outcome.

What does daily planning on a team scale actually look like? For my colleague, it means never setting a meeting for a small, nit-picking topic but instead being considerate of her teams' time by utilizing already-established meeting times to the fullest. During *brief* daily team meetings (usually held in the morning), she provides important updates and news to the team and uses the opportunity to poll the group on real-time issues, including them in the decision-making process. Instead of having a lengthy and jam-packed monthly or weekly meeting, where folks inevitably tune out, she tackles what is the most important in scheduled times each day. It's much more manageable for the team as individuals than if they dumped the month's goals on them in one hour-long session.

Suddenly, hitting the quota for the month doesn't seem as daunting when your team's daily goals are so manageable. In addition, daily planning as a team puts the importance of each person's role and contributions into perspective. It showcases each person's value and gives everyone something to focus on. Daily planning from a team perspective also cuts down on unnecessary drama and workplace distractions by making each person aware of their colleagues' unique insights. Team members feel heard and others become aware of their contributions. Teams that plan together succeed together!

---

**Daily planning as a team puts the importance of each person's role and contributions into perspective.**

---

## MAKE THE EVENING WORK FOR YOU

If you've been putting out fires all day, chances are that when the evening rolls around, you have no energy left to expend on important things. However, when you start planning your days based on the rewards you will reap — focused on achievements and milestones not firefighting and busy-ness — suddenly you can enjoy evenings that serve you better. Just like mornings, evenings are different for everyone. Depending on the season, my evenings can range from being spent on the road for business, in the stands at a ball field, at home, or anywhere in between. Depending on your industry, evenings could mean a shift change, closing the doors, or just getting started.

Ask yourself: "Are your evenings working for you?" Time spent in the evenings can make the next day easier or harder. If you find that you lack time in the mornings, it may be because you are trying to do too much — things you could have started the night before. Things like tidying up, laying out clothes, and preparing meals for the next day are more effective when done the night before. And daily planning of your workday can typically be done the night before as well! If flexible morning hours aren't an option, then the evening may offer a more flexible time to navigate whatever change you're facing. Maybe instead of facing your inbox in the middle of the workday, you set aside evening hours to respond to everyone. Can you add in 30 minutes of reading — for enjoyment or professional growth, or both — to your evening routine?

What about when your evenings are filled with commitments? How do you navigate those precious evening hours? For me, my evening hours are often spent on a ball field watching my sons play sports. This is a non-negotiable commitment for me because I value taking the time to help them grow and develop. There are lots of things I'd *like* to do in the evenings but making sure I say "yes" to the things that matter the most to me is how I make sure I use my time wisely and how I stay true to myself. Changes you're making may require that you use time in the evenings to relax and recharge your batteries. If you are saying "yes" to too many things, you could be sabotaging your own needs. Perhaps you are spending too much time relaxing and not enough working toward your goals. Or maybe you're spending too much time volunteering and participating in civic events, which leaves little time for yourself or your family. Or perhaps you never really step away from your work, and it's bleeding significantly into your evenings. Whatever the case may be, make sure the way you spend your evenings helps you to achieve an overall healthy balance.

There are all sorts of excuses regarding our time and how we use it. Remember, you have the same hours in a day as the most successful person on the planet. It's up to you as to how you use them. Change requires that you get out of your comfort zone and your evening routine is no exception. Take time each evening to reflect on your day. What things did you accomplish? What was left over that you need to work on tomorrow? What upcoming events or projects need extra attention? Planning and reflecting doesn't mean leaving no room for spontaneity and adventure. Instead, it gives us tools to ensure we have time for all that matters most to us.

I've seen so many unique ways individuals and teams plan their days. Personally, I like to use a formatted daily planner that allows me to carry over from one day to the next and include my hourly schedule. I recently switched to a digital format that allows me to link my Outlook calendar to tasks and notes. Don't be afraid to try new planning tools and methods. How you plan needs to be flexible enough to change along with you! Some of my colleagues plan hour-by-hour in digital calendars. Some plans are intricate and detailed while others are concise and simple. The ability to leverage change individually or as a team comes from how you spend the 1,440 minutes you are given each day, and always remembering that you are in the driver's seat; you're in charge of your time and you alone have control and power over how you spend it. As for how your time-management decisions impact others, remember that you don't have to have a title to be a leader. Sometimes setting the example is all that's needed to spark something positive within your organization. Start with yourself and manage your own time in a way that serves you or even liberates you. Odds are that others will take notice of the positive impact stemming from your efforts to plan each day with intention.

# MAP YOUR DAY

What am I grateful for today?

**Top Three Priorities for the Day:**

1. _____

2. _____

3. _____

**My schedule:**

8:00 a.m. _____

9:00 a.m. _____

10:00 a.m. _____

11:00 a.m. _____

12:00 p.m. _____

1:00 p.m. _____

2:00 p.m. _____

3:00 p.m. _____

4:00 p.m. _____

5:00 p.m. _____

6:00 p.m. _____

7:00 p.m. _____

8:00 p.m. _____

**Reflect: What did you accomplish today? What will you need to work on tomorrow?**

_____

_____

_____

_____

_____

_____

## CHAPTER 9

# At the Crossroads

*The road has ended*
*But I feel lost.*
*I thought I'd be happy*
*After so much time, work, and cost.*
*The destination seemed nice*
*When I saw pictures in the brochure.*
*But upon arrival,*
*I'm not so sure.*
*The grass looked green*
*But instead is brown;*
*I have to turn this car around.*
*A signal, a shift.*
*And off I go ...*
*The journey is half the fun,*
*You know!*

In work and in life, we will approach many a crossroads — where we find ourselves looking left and right, ahead and behind, trying to decide if it's prudent to keep heading straight or if it's time to make a turn. Big changes and decision points are proverbial crossroads. And it helps to have a strategy and a clear mindset about how you'll approach the intersections of life. Not every change is worth navigating and not every path worth traveling in the long run. If you're like most of us, you will sometimes recognize that a choice you have made is no longer serving you. If your choices have put you on a path you don't want to be on anymore, then it's time to select the ideal crossroad and turn.

Veering off the road to venture a different direction requires taking a leap of faith, which can be a scary proposition. On one hand, it's something you may want to do and strongly feel that it will improve your life. On the other hand, there may be variables and unknowns that keep you from turning the wheel. Making a turn may mean changing jobs or career trajectories, breaking away from toxic relationships, or simply leaving behind whatever is no longer serving you. If making a turn is something you've been considering, here are a few steps that might put everything into perspective.

# FIRST, BE HONEST WITH YOURSELF

I have had the unique privilege of working with many people in varying professions. I recently had a conversation with a friend who works in sales. Having been recently promoted, he was feeling overwhelmed in his new position. While he was happy to have received the promotion, the responsibilities were greater than he anticipated. What was his solution? To seek yet another promotion. This position was higher ranking and included a larger office space. In his mind, the private office space is what would give him the edge and allow him to work more efficiently. He had convinced himself that the shiny new office and upgraded title would magically alleviate his worries. He hadn't thought about all the additional stress the new role might carry. Like the promotion he just received, another advancement would come with added responsibility and a greater workload. Roles with added perks also come with added stress and responsibility. How could others expect him to be happy with *that* role if he was unhappy in his current role? He was falling victim to "the grass is always greener" mentality. My advice to him? Don't fall victim to seeking titles or accolades but, instead, give yourself time to adjust and build your skills. He was in a transitional phase, where his discomfort would inevitably turn to growth. He just needed to be honest with himself and admit that the discomfort he was facing would not be alleviated by a shiny new office and *more* responsibility. Being honest with yourself cultivates growth.

---

## Being honest with yourself cultivates growth.

---

Sometimes we want something so badly that we convince ourselves that it's what is best for us. This is especially the case if we're talking about something we've invested lots of time or money into, or if it's something we have a strong emotional attachment to (e.g., something tied to our ego or pride, our sense of value, our passion or sweet spot). Often, we ignore our gut and continue to press on in circumstances that aren't making us (or won't ever make us) truly happy. To break away from this cycle, we first must be honest with ourselves. As I've gotten older, I find that the ability to be completely honest with myself is so important. Being able to admit to yourself your true motives behind your actions is powerful. Only when you are truly honest and accepting of yourself will you begin to see opportunities that align with what makes you happy. Ask yourself if the situation you are in aligns with your values and goals. Our personal values play a huge part in how we perceive what's around us. If what we are doing and surrounding ourselves with every day conflicts with our personal value systems, then we are setting ourselves up for failure.

---

**If what we are doing and surrounding ourselves with every day conflicts with our personal value systems, then we are setting ourselves up for failure.**

---

Think about your goals. Does your current situation align with and set you up for success toward your personal goals? If your personal goals are to be happy and stress-free but you're involving yourself in petty office politics, then you're working against yourself. By now, if you have mapped out your goals and thought about what it will take to achieve them, you've likely got a pretty good idea if your current situation is going to get you there. If the circumstances you find yourself in now aren't going to get you where you'd like to be, then it's time to look for a crossroads and turn. To do that, you must be extremely honest with yourself and unafraid to face uncomfortable truths.

It's okay to take some time to find the right place to turn. Weigh the "pros and cons" of the change you're considering. Put it down on paper. Map out ways that you can overcome the cons for yourself. Making significant changes is hard! The cons can be huge factors, like finances, where you live, and relationships. They shouldn't be taken lightly but you should consider everything with the bigger picture in mind. Weigh each component against your personal values, goals, and what's meaningful to *you*. What you're considering may not be a change, but instead choosing *not* to make or support a change. You may determine that an unwelcome change goes against that which you value and that's okay. Knowing how to determine what is important to you, and how to align your choices with that, is key to staying on the right path for yourself.

If you are part of an organization facing changes, the same principle holds true. Honesty first. You and your coworkers must be honest with yourselves about the impact changes will have. Knowing potential problems is the first step to building awesome solutions! It doesn't do your supervisors, leaders, or colleagues any good for you to tell them what you think they want to hear. Be brave, be respectful, be open, and be a part of the solution!

# BE HONEST WITH OTHERS

If you've decided to make a turn or take a detour, then one of the most difficult steps is to be honest with others and tell them how you're feeling. It could be a conversation with a colleague, friend, family member, or anyone who is directly involved in your current situation. You might be afraid that people will not understand your decision to make a change and won't be supportive. However, you'll never know if you don't take the time to be honest and let people know what you're thinking, feeling, and planning. It's usually true that the fear and worry about doing something is greater than the discomfort of actually doing it. Be brave and decide to share.

When I was younger, I would spend so much time "editing" myself to fit in. I am an inherently unfiltered individual in a world that seems to demand filters, so this was an exhausting practice. In addition, others can sense when you aren't being genuine, which only pushes them away. It wasn't until I started embracing my quirks and unfiltered self that others did too. You aren't doing anyone any favors by hiding parts of yourself. In times of change, your unique contribution could be *exactly* what everyone needs! One of the coolest things about finally being honest with others regarding change is that you can be pleasantly surprised by the responses. Often, the fear of sharing with others is completely unnecessary. Being honest can open doors to greater opportunities, better communication, healing, and better relationships. Share your reasons, listen to feedback, and be prepared for critique, but understand that it isn't personal. Be ready for questions and listen with the intent to understand the other person's perspective. They may share insights that help you on your journey and offer support you didn't expect. Being honest with those around you brings clarity to the road and challenges ahead.

---

**Being honest with those around you brings clarity to the road and challenges ahead.**

---

When I was considering changing careers, I decided to mention it to a colleague of mine — a fellow elementary school teacher. I had built it up so much in my mind — this idea of "quitting" being a teacher — that I was prepared to hear only negatives. I knew they would tell me I was crazy, I'd never work in the field again, I'd be giving up a steady income, and so on. I worried to the point that telling someone else was eating away at me. When I finally shared my thoughts, feelings, and plans, my colleague was completely supportive. She shared stories with me about a similar change she had made and how she was still thankful she had done it. She put into perspective all the things I thought I was *losing*, by reminding me of all I had to *gain*. That conversation changed the trajectory of my career. I'm still thankful that I overcame my fear of talking to her, and I'm thankful to *her* for her support.

# BE BRAVE

Taking a leap of faith, veering off course, and breaking free of what isn't serving you takes a whole lotta' bravery! It is scary. It requires staring each fear in the face and creating a plan to overcome it. How brave have you been lately? Have you been making choices based on growth or based on comfort? When we've been honest with ourselves, understood our values and goals, and taken the time to let others in, then being brave and going for it is the final step.

---

## How brave have you been lately? Have you been making choices based on growth or based on comfort?

---

Once you've taken the time to understand how you got where you are, whether it aligns with your values and goals, and what it will take to change, the only thing left to do is jump! Bravery isn't something we're all born with. Even once I overcame my fear of the water, I was never the kid to run and cannonball into the pool. I always started with the tip of my toe, then my foot, followed by both feet, and so on. I eased my way into my courageous moments. The only way to build our own bravery up is to keep doing things that make us uncomfortable. As Dory says in *Finding Nemo*, "Just keep swimming!"

In another context, I have worked with countless individuals who have great ideas for their organization but feel too afraid to share. They don't feel afraid because others have made them feel that way, but because of their own assumptions and insecurities. Speculating and assuming how something will go is a practice that only leads to poor results. If you are operating from an honest place and you want the best for your organization, then don't be afraid to share (respectfully) your thoughts with the appropriate audience. Great ideas belong in the boardroom, not the breakroom.

Think of bravery as a tank. If you're starting out with a low or empty tank, you won't make it very far. Each time you step out of your comfort zone, even a little, the experience slowly fills your tank with bravery. Navigating pros and cons of the change with yourself adds a little to the tank. Discussing your goals with someone else adds a little to the tank. Researching, aligning, and making small changes add even more. The more you let go of autopilot, take control of your choices, and take small steps toward your goals, the more you add to your bravery tank each time. Slowly but surely, each small step out of your comfort zone fills your bravery tank ever so slightly. Eventually, your bravery tank will be full and you'll be ready to take that leap!

# BRAVERY TANK

**How full is your bravery tank? (Fill in the gauge.)**

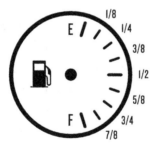

**Name three things you can do to step out of your comfort zone (a little) and fill your tank.**

1. _____

2. _____

3. _____

**Reflect: How did it go? What did you learn?**

_____

_____

_____

_____

_____

_____

## CHAPTER 10

# The Carpool Effect

*I planted a seed*
*And then it grew.*
*Before I knew it,*
*There were two.*
*A plant, a row,*
*A row, a field ...*
*Who knew how much this change would yield?*

The amazing thing about navigating change successfully is that you not only see immediate results, but the entire process is contagious. Reaching your beautiful destination just makes other folks want to come along for the ride! So much of what we avoid due to fear ends up being *exactly* what other people need to drive them forward. Being able to share your story and help others do the same makes the entire journey rewarding. In this chapter, I want to encourage you to be vulnerable, brave, and look for ways to leverage the change you've navigated to be of service to others.

# SPECTATORS

Like it or not, someone is always watching. And people with watchful eyes are often judgmental. My mother always told me that the *right* choice wasn't always the most *popular* choice. Changing is always sure to attract attention, and not always the good kind. We hear a lot about culture within organizations, but culture exists within all types of relationships. Accepting and embracing change for ourselves typically has a large effect and, as such, others are apt to take notice. Your change has the potential to inspire others along the way. Even the most resistant of folks can be brought around by observing your story. Nothing ever seems as hard if we've watched another person move through it with success. With that comes a greater responsibility to share your momentum with others when they are ready.

Not long ago, I was watching a popular reality television clip in which a husband and wife were discussing some problems they'd been facing. The wife had made the positive change of getting healthier and losing a substantial amount of weight. She set a goal and met it. To her, she had reason to celebrate. The husband, however, wasn't ready for the change. The weight loss made him feel like he was with a stranger. He felt like the change, while positive, had fractured their relationship. They were at an impasse. The wife didn't need to gain her weight back, but the husband was having a hard time adjusting. This made me think. How many times are positive changes made harder because the effects weren't something others were ready for?

The same ripple effect that inspires others to make positive changes can, conversely, sometimes cause people to distance themselves. Others aren't always ready for the changes you accept, and that's okay. We must remember where we started and extend the same grace to others who aren't quite there yet. Giving grace to others also reaffirms the positive changes you've made and makes them visible in a different way. When you accept and embrace change, the ripples can reach far and wide. It is amazing to watch how a change can uplift others ... who then "share the love" by embracing changes themselves.

I believe that wherever you are now, embracing change is the secret to getting where you want to go. And I'm convinced that the best part about the journey is the "passengers" — those other people you get to inspire and take along for the ride! Being brave and having the courage to conquer whatever is in front of you gives permission to others to do the same. Whether the change is a personal or an organizational one, navigating an important change becomes a tool to empower more than just yourself. There is a certain confidence that only comes from making significant positive changes. Just imagine the collective impact you can have by leveraging your experiences to help others do the same.

------------------

### I believe that wherever you are now, embracing change is the secret to getting where you want to go.

------------------

As a corporate trainer, I've had the unique privilege of working for various organizations facing unique changes. Often, organizational changes require team members to make personal changes as well. For example, a change in structure may lead to changes in leadership that cause reporting issues for frontline team members. Process changes can speed things up or slow things down and create changes in hours needed to complete projects. Changing hours cause personal changes with childcare or home life that may not have been anticipated in the "big picture" thinking that initiated the change. Alternatively, most of us aren't able to simply shed stress from work when we go home. Inevitably, we carry especially hard days home with us and the tension may overflow to our partner, children, or other family members. Things like this can leave team members feeling overwhelmed and alone. Remember that one bright light can illuminate a dark room. When you have successfully navigated change, you can now be that light for others. You are now able to meet others in the trenches, so to speak, and help them discover solutions and make lasting changes of their own. You can turn a difficult situation into a positive experience for all. Think of it as "the carpool effect," which has five distinct advantages.

# CARPOOLING ADVANTAGE #1

## An Opportunity to Position Yourself for Visibility and Impact

Serving others is one of the greatest privileges we are given in this life. When you have successfully navigated change for yourself, being able to help others do the same is extremely rewarding. The beautiful thing about serving is that it's something you can do no matter where you are. You don't need a title or permission. All you need is a willingness to position yourself where you can be of service. Look at your immediate surroundings:

- Can you help others navigate change at work?
- What about at church or a local school?
- Are there civic organizations in your organization where you can volunteer your time to help them through transitional periods?

It may seem presumptuous to offer help during times of change at work if you haven't been asked. However, many managers will tell you that those who volunteer without being asked are more likely to be promoted. Volunteering to help managers or your leadership team navigate workplace changes will likely be a welcomed effort with lasting payoff.

---

**Volunteering to help managers or your leadership team navigate workplace changes will likely be a welcomed effort with lasting payoff.**

---

Be observant of the small ways an organizational change is having ripple effects. Do you recognize a way a process can be improved? Vocalize solutions and watch as you become everyone's new best friend! During times of organizational change, there is never a shortage of folks sharing why things don't work and pointing out all the problems. For every problem or negative you hear, write down 3-5 simple solutions or workarounds. Position yourself in the areas of greatest need and watch as you share solutions and become everyone's new best friend!

# CARPOOLING ADVANTAGE #2

## Sharing Your Journey Builds Credibility and Creates Connection

Your experiences and words of wisdom *matter*! It's easy to discount your own perspective but sharing your own change journey can have a powerful effect on others. Sometimes just knowing that someone has made it through a difficult change is inspiration enough. Being vulnerable with others can sometimes feel like weakness but is, in fact, one of our greatest strengths. Lettings others know where we have struggled creates deeper connections and makes us so much more relatable. Brené Brown says, "You either walk inside your story and own it or you stand outside your story and hustle for your worthiness." Being brave enough to share your story gives you a level of credibility that nothing else can.

---

Being vulnerable with others can sometimes feel like weakness but is, in fact, one of our greatest strengths.

---

# CARPOOLING ADVANTAGE #3

## Repaving the Highway Creates Smooth Travels for Us All

I once worked for an organization with a culture of anxiety and cynicism. Everyone was stressed and burned out, had become catty and petty, and the overall vibe was just awful. The energy inside the organization was perpetually negative. What should have been a great place to work — because it offered good hours, fair pay, and generous benefits — was a place everyone despised. I was new and very hesitant to speak up or ruffle any feathers for fear of not fitting in or being accepted. One day, during a typical staff meeting, everyone was discussing an issue. All around the table, every comment was either an excuse to deflect blame or an accusation intended to assign blame. About halfway through the meeting, one of my coworkers, who I did not know very well at the time, spoke up with something altogether surprising. Instead of going along with the negativity, she shared her story. She spoke from a place of honesty about how she had been struggling to enjoy her job and thought all the negative talk was really taking a toll on how she felt. She then shared that she would be participating in a "no complaining" challenge for the next 30 days and encouraged everyone else to do the same.

Well, let's talk about a total "mic drop moment." At that point, everyone shared a small sentiment then continued with their day. Many rolled their eyes as we left the meeting, expressing cynicism. Plenty were quick to point out that she had been just as negative as they were. They saw her about-face in attitude as hypocrisy. Do you want to know what I saw? I saw someone stepping out in bravery. She noticed something that needed to *change* — in herself and in others — so she shared her story to change the narrative and the energy in the room. She didn't make it about anyone else and instead shared her own perspective and her personal goals.

While everyone was cynical at first (and, really, who wouldn't be?), over the next few weeks her lack of complaining led to others trying the challenge too. Slowly but surely, not complaining started to brighten the mood of the entire organization. Even those who were the most cynical and biggest eye-rollers eventually complained less and less. Our next meeting was altogether different. People started sharing praises and helping others. That woman, who is now a dear friend, probably has no idea the impact she had on others. The entire environment had changed simply because she was brave and shared her story. Along the path of change, she had repaved the potholes and made a smoother ride for us all. And doing so was quite simple.

Sharing your story is not only valuable to others but is also one of those steps that fills your bravery tank (see Chapter 9). It takes bravery to be vulnerable and share with others. Each time you do, you keep adding to that bravery tank. You are taking ownership over your story and your choices, and you are reminding yourself of what you're capable of. Your story of change is a light to keep you going when things seem dark. The beautiful thing about that light is what a beacon it can become for others as well. There is power in sharing your story.

# CARPOOLING ADVANTAGE #4

## When We Change Together, Human Empathy Can Transform Us

Times of change are also times of high emotion for most people. Whether the change is a planned organizational change or a change tied to achieving a personal goal, times of change can be times of difficult transition. Conflicts, changes in mood, and the need to vent frustrations tend to increase. As such, it's vital that we use empathy when talking to others; empathy, when received by others, helps them feel seen and heard. Resist the temptation to advise from your perspective unless the other person is open and remember what it felt like when you were in a period of transition. When emotions are high, it can be difficult to uncover true feelings. People can appear to be upset about one thing but something else may be the root of the problem. When we take time to really listen as someone talks through those emotions, we uncover so much more about the real problems they may be facing.

When emotions are high, we are wired to let our emotions respond in kind — amped up, extreme, without thought. What a surprise it is to someone experiencing high emotions when we instead respond with empathy and compassion. That negative coworker you deal with, they likely need the empathy and grace the most. I'm super sassy by nature so this is a flex for me. When someone comes at me with high emotions, it is really hard for me not to get on the same wavelength. However, that response hasn't historically yielded the best results. I once had a colleague come to me with a lot of negativity and criticism that was out of character for them. It very much felt like a personal attack and every fiber of my being wanted to respond in anger. In the moment, I was hurt and felt very depleted. I walked away from the conversation without responding harshly. Instead,

I took away everything they had to say and instead thought about where that was coming from. After all, people don't take things out on others for no reason.

I ultimately decided that my colleague must have been feeling small, frustrated, and generally down on themselves. If not, they wouldn't have been trying to make me feel the same way. What did I decide to do? I sent that colleague a message letting them know what a great job they were doing and how much I appreciated them. Even though I was hurt and angry, I knew responding with anger wouldn't solve the ultimate problem. That colleague reached back out to me to let me know how much they appreciated and needed that message. I found out they had indeed been having a difficult week and desperately needed to hear uplifting words! That singular interaction strengthened our relationship and built trust between us. Start seeing times of high emotion as opportunities to break down walls and respond with empathy. The results are worth it!

---

**Start seeing times of high emotion as opportunities to break down walls and respond with empathy.**

---

# CARPOOLING ADVANTAGE #5

## Together, We Can Celebrate Small Wins

Change is a process that requires a lot of motivation and will power. Take time to not only celebrate small wins for yourself but for others as well. Be someone who notices and acknowledges the efforts of others. Everyone needs to know that what they're doing is seen and valued. People who face change with support and encouragement are much more likely to reach success than those who are met with rules, deadlines, and criticism. Remember what it was like as *you* were navigating change and be for others what you needed during that time.

---

**People who face change with support and encouragement are much more likely to reach success than those who are met with rules, deadlines, and criticism.**

---

I once asked a successful manager how they managed to meet goals and keep morale high. It was simple: "We don't wait until the goal is met to celebrate. We celebrate all the time." From shout-outs to praises on work accomplishments and personal accomplishments, absolutely nothing was off-limits for a celebration to this manager. Even the most standard, work-related meeting became a time for celebration and fellowship. Despite being workers in an incredibly busy business with loads to be stressed about, her people were happy and looked forward to their day. Her team felt loved and appreciated because they were constantly celebrated. Celebration had become a language to them, where each team member constantly encouraged and praised others for the work they were doing and things going on in their lives. Aside from making it an awesome place to work, that positive energy trickled down to their customers in the community and made a *huge* impact! It also increased their business. This manager and her people weren't just meeting goals ... they were exceeding them!

I've had managers tell me that they shouldn't have to constantly praise people. They feel like people should do a good job because they are paid to do so. They see the need for praise as a weakness in others. They may think it's a generational need, something silly that "those young folks" constantly seek. Many business consultants, speakers, and authors have made lots of money dissecting each generation's quirks, and while I think these analyses are worthwhile, I happen to believe we *all* need praise — regardless of when we were born. Having worked with multiple people spanning several generations, I can honestly say that *everyone* needs to be celebrated. Any team member will do more without being asked if they know that what they do is meaningful to someone else. So many workplace changes could be made easier if managers, supervisors, and leaders would take time to celebrate small wins. And when it comes to a return on investment, celebrating small wins can't be beat. It costs absolutely nothing and increases workplace production exponentially. Better still, you don't have to wait on a manager or supervisor to celebrate. *you* can be the celebrator in your environment. Celebrate *everything*!

---

So many workplace changes could be made easier if managers, supervisors, and leaders would take time to celebrate small wins. And when it comes to a return on investment, celebrating small wins can't be beat.

---

Celebrating small wins also means giving one another grace to make mistakes and try again. Change is messy and difficult, yet so rewarding. Take time to celebrate the fact that you or someone else just *tried*! Trying to navigate any change is better than resisting or giving up. Sometimes the failure is worth celebrating as much as the success because we learn more from it. The more we fail, the more we learn, and the more we grow. Celebrate the effort and the failures! When we feel safe enough to fail and are encouraged to keep going, we *all* succeed!

# THE ROAD AHEAD

**What change have you successfully navigated?**

_____

_____

_____

**How did you or how will you celebrate?**

_____

_____

_____

**What did you learn from the process that could help someone else?**

_____

_____

_____

**List three people you plan to encourage this week.**

1. _____

2. _____

3. _____

# CONCLUSION

---

# The Never-Ending Journey

The remarkable and most difficult part of the change journey is that the road keeps on coming. Sometimes it's straight and smooth, but sometimes it's winding and dangerous. It's easy to veer off course, grow tired, and want to give up. Change is broad, constant, welcome, unwelcome, difficult, and necessary. I want to encourage you to keep on going. The road will take you, your goals, your dreams, and your teams to amazing places if you let it. The key is to let it.

Change is never easy. Whether the change you are facing is at work or at home, voluntary or involuntary, you can leverage it to accomplish whatever goals you have. By embracing change and getting out of your comfort zone, you'll feel positive impacts for yourself and set an example for others. Becoming self-aware and taking ownership for your mindset, choices, and actions enables you to break barriers and live the life you dream of. Keep changing, keep growing, and keep navigating this wild road called life!

# KEEP GOING

It is inevitable — especially when facing a change that you didn't ask for — that you may run out of gas. The road may get too long, and you may feel like you won't ever reach the destination. Sometimes when one change starts, it leads to several more and it can seem like too much change to manage. If you feel like you're running out of gas, I urge you to revisit Chapter 3's discussion of how to reset and rejuvenate yourself. Remember, it's completely okay to check your mirrors, slow down, and use a map to help you determine your direction. You may even need that time to decide if you want to stay on the road you're on or take a turn at the next intersection.

If you're in an organization struggling with change, remember that assessing and focusing on the mindset of your people, recognizing your Change Embracers, and giving grace will make the entire process a lot easier. Realize that organizational changes translate to personal changes for a lot of people and nothing is as simple as it seems. For the most part, people aim to please and they only set out on the Path of Resistance when they feel they haven't been heard or they're coping with unresolved fears. Take time to discover who within your organization could use some extra TLC. Not a manager? That's okay. You don't have to be. In times of change, true leaders emerge by helping those around them navigate the changes.

If you are someone stuck "backseat driving" for your organization — judging, criticizing, and naysaying without offering to help — take time to understand how the change was necessary and do what you can to understand how your perspective is impacting your resistance to the change. If the change isn't directly challenging your personal beliefs or values, then plan to break it apart and tackle it day by day. You'll be amazed at how your journey will inspire others.

If you're seeking to embrace change for yourself, then bravo! We aren't wired to love change from the start but learning the magic behind leveraging it makes for one exciting journey! It takes practice and you may have to revisit the lessons and exercises in this book often while you are perfecting your map and plotting your destinations. If there ever was a guaranteed way of getting the most out of life's twists and turns by improving your teams or yourself, navigating, embracing, and leveraging change is it! I'm so proud of you and excited for the journey you are on!

Until we meet again ...

# EPILOGUE

---

# Warning: Detour!

*Shew wee, y'all!* (Yes, that is the most southern phrase I have typed in this book.) When I started writing *Buckle Up, Buttercup!* in 2018, I had no idea just how much change the world would soon be facing or how timely the messages in my book would become when the book released in 2020. As someone who typically champions change and helps others navigate it, I found myself in unchartered territory. The COVID-19 pandemic has brought a whole new meaning to "navigating change" by thrusting massive amounts of unwelcome changes on everyone. Everything about our daily lives has been turned upside down. From personal health crisis or concerns to job loss, remote work structure, school and childcare closures, limited resources across multiple industries, our healthcare system being stretched to its max, and the sudden loss of social everything, I had to stop and redirect more than once (despite being a true Change Embracer who tries to practice what she preaches).

I know we won't be in this forever. In the South, you might hear: "This too shall pass. It might pass like a kidney stone, but it *will* pass." Indeed, what the world has dealt with during the coronavirus pandemic has created change on an immeasurable scale. I wrote this book to help folks navigate professional and personal change and make the most of it. In light of the pandemic, and before saying farewell as you close the final pages of this book, I'd like to reiterate a few thoughts that I suspect you might need to hear:

1. **It's okay not to be okay.** Change is such a broad term. When I have suggested strategies for dealing with change in this book, I am referring to those personal and professional changes that can hold us back from achieving our goals. The changes people have faced (and will likely face for years or even decades) due to the pandemic go far beyond that. Many are catastrophic losses that will take years to recover from, if ever. Don't expect too much from yourself if these are the types of changes you are facing. Sometimes putting your foot on the brake instead of the gas is the right choice. Give yourself grace. It's okay not to be okay.

2. **Compassion makes change easier.** Mary Poppins recommended that a spoonful of sugar would make medicine easier to swallow. In that same spirit, the world needs kindness and compassion now more than ever. Neighbors, friends, colleagues, and family members are seeing their normal lives swept away in an instant. At the time this book headed to press, more than 90,000 Americans had died from the virus. In times of insurmountable change, the world needs your kindness, generosity, and every ounce of compassion you can muster. The greatest lessons I have learned regarding change in the pandemic is that all the worldly things we cling to can be stripped away, canceled,

and plucked from our lives instantly but love, faith, compassion for one another, and community will endure.

3. **We *all* need help sometimes.** Even if we like to think so, we seldom do things alone. Often, somewhere along the journey, someone was there to lend a helping hand. During the pandemic I have seen folks help in amazing and surprising ways. Checking in on the elderly, delivering groceries, volunteering at health-care facilities, and making donations are some of the ways I've witnessed people come together and help one another. I've been on the receiving end of grace from my employer, as I found myself without childcare when schools closed and social distancing was enforced. I don't know anyone who the pandemic has not touched in some way.

I hope that wherever you are, and whatever you are facing — whether you read this book in the immediate aftermath of the coronavirus crisis or many years hence — this book helps you to make the most of the situation you've been dealt. For many, a new journey is now beginning. Proceed with care and caution. The light ahead may be red, yellow, or green but the world needs you to stay in the race. Changes big and small need navigating and how you steer through will chart a brave new course for yourself and others. I hope this book brings you hope. *Buckle Up, Buttercup!* Stay in the driver's seat whenever you can, be a cheerleader and not a backseat driver when you're on the periphery, and know that you are full of strength and potential and value, today and always. Keep driving.

# ACKNOWLEDGMENTS

To **Seth** – Thank you for loving me, supporting me, and being my safe place to land. I love you the most.

To **Mom and Dad** – Thank you for being the best family a girl could ask for, teaching me to dream big, work hard, and never give up.

To **Jac** – Thanks for being the best sister who always wipes away all my self-doubt.

To **Nana and Papa** – Thank you for loving my kiddos and always supporting me.

To **Jimmy, Alex, Suzanne, and my entire First Southern family** – Thank you for planting me, breathing wisdom into me, and giving me room to grow.

To **Cole and Case** – I love you both more than words can express. You are forever and always my *why*. Thanks for making me brave.

To the **Silver Tree Publishing** team, **Kate Colbert, Stephanie Feger, Penny Tate, and Courtney Hudson** – Thank you for turning a dream into a reality and helping me discover the power of my voice.

To **Abby** – Thank you for, in all times, being the truest friend.

To **Christy Phelps** – Thanks for being an exceptional teacher who told me I should be published one day. I listened.

# GO BEYOND THE BOOK

Overwhelmed and need someone else to grab the wheel? No problem! From simple brainstorming to strategic plans, let Michelle Wyatt tailor a plan to your needs.

**To learn more, visit:**

🌐     BuckleUpButtercupTheBook.com

**Have a unique proposal or question? Michelle would love to hear it!**

✉️     Michelle@Michelle-Wyatt.com

**Want more? Find articles and free resources on navigating professional change:**

in     LinkedIn.com/in/Michelle-Wyatt-Author

# ABOUT THE AUTHOR

Credit: Kate Phelps Photography

Michelle Wyatt is passionate about helping teams and individuals find success by learning to embrace, navigate, and leverage change. By sharing the change management techniques used to navigate a huge career change for herself, Michelle helps others gain a deeper understanding of what makes change so scary and how to overcome those fears. She works with individuals seeking to make meaningful change and organizations looking to help their teams embrace change, using proven techniques and activities to propel everyone forward.

Michelle began her career as a primary school teacher with a graduate degree in K-5 Teacher Leadership and has found her niche as a corporate trainer, most recently with First Southern Bancorp. She lives in Western Kentucky with her husband, Seth, and two sons, Cole and Case. *Buckle Up, Buttercup!* is her first nonfiction book.

Made in the USA
Monee, IL
26 May 2020

31951467R00098